Somerville

MASSACHUSETTS

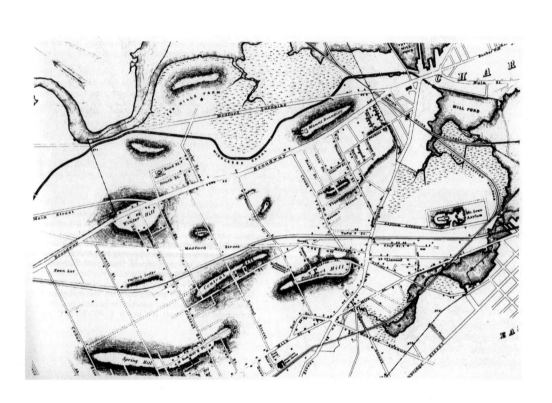

Somerville

MASSACHUSETTS

A BRIEF HISTORY

Dee Morris and Dora St. Martin

Charleston | London

THE
History
PRESS

Published by The History Press
Charleston, SC 29403
www.historypress.net

Cover image: Postcard, Somerville Theatre, 1914.

All images are courtesy of the authors unless otherwise noted.

First published 2008

Manufactured in the United Kingdom

ISBN 978.1.59629.424.0

Library of Congress Cataloging-in-Publication Data

Morris, Dee.
Somerville : a brief history / Dee Morris and Dora St. Martin.
p. cm.
Includes bibliographical references and index.
ISBN 978-1-59629-424-0
1. Somerville (Mass.)--History. I. St. Martin, Dora. II. Title.
F74.S7M67 2008
974.4'4--dc22
                            2008019189

"But there are cities that are still dear to us above all others, because they are what I may call cities of the heart. There we are born, there we have lived, there our little lot in life was cast, there is the spot where our fortunes or our characters have been nurtured…and the scenes amid which have sprung up some of the tenderest and most sacred ties. To most of us Somerville is such a spot."
   —Reverend William H. Pierson, 1892

"Somerville doesn't have to tip its hat to anybody in the country as far as history goes. We're older than Boston, and our history dwarfs Cambridge. Somerville is a tiny city geographically but a big city when it comes to population. That adds up to a lot of stories."
   —Bob "Monty" Doherty, of the Somerville Fire Department, 2007

Contents

Acknowledgements

We would like to thank those who helped us in their professional capacities: Kevin O'Kelly, Ron Castile and the staff of the Somerville Public Library; Jeanne Gamble of Historic New England; and the staff of the Boston Public Library.

We would like to thank individuals for their kindness in loaning us family photographs, personal artwork and stories: Joanne Cook, Ed Dente, Bob "Monty" Doherty, Charlie McCarthy, the families of Maynard and Laverne Bachelder and Marie (Marchi) Bonello and past and present members of the Somerville Historical Society.

We would like to thank our family and friends, especially Joleen and Laura Collins, Karen Hohler and Alonzo and Sarah Eliot for their good-natured encouragement and support.

Finally, we would like to thank John Martin for his technical expertise and support, without whom this book would not look so pretty.

Introduction

Somerville is 4.2 square miles of hills, neighborhoods and people. It is a place where the concept of community is vital, yet individuality is treasured. Somerville is constantly changing and is always in a state of becoming. Next door to Boston, it is a natural gateway used by countless generations as a convenient place to live. But the city's fluid nature cannot be explained away so easily. We discovered some of its complexity and contradictions as we put together educational and historical programs.

Making history come alive is always a challenge. In our many Victorian walking tours of Somerville, we have had the joy of introducing our contemporaries to their neighbors from the past. As we learned about these former residents, we were amazed at their drive to improve their lives and to take responsibility for their community. We have found, paraphrasing Shakespeare, that some were born great, some achieved greatness and some had greatness thrust upon them. They changed the expectations for themselves and, as a result, changed a city.

Our book flows chronologically through the eyes of these Victorians—looking back to the Revolutionary past, yet daring to embrace a future filled with new inventions. It is not history in a straight line. Somerville's hills act as bookmarks to represent key times, events and directions in the city's history:

Ten Hills Farm, home to the earliest settlers and the state's first governor;
Cobble Hill, where General Putnam placed his cannon during the siege of Boston and later McLean Asylum for the Insane;
Ploughed Hill (also called Mount Benedict), where religion and race played out in the burning of the Ursuline Convent;
Middle Hill (also known as Central Hill), named because it stands in the center of the other prominences, but is also core to Somerville's civic life;
Winter Hill, once crowned with elegant mansions and later home to a streetcar suburb and a growing merchant class;
elegant *Spring Hill*, where women found their voices;
Prospect Hill and *Union Square*, where the flying of the first flag made history and inspired a generation of writers;

Workmen construct Washington Street while admiring citizens look on. *Somerville Annual Report, 1901.*

Workmen spread asphalt on Cross Street. *Somerville Annual Report, 1901.*

Clarendon and *Wild Cat Hills*, bordering Cambridge and last to be developed, playing host to a Civil War camp and Somerville's African American community;

Quarry and *Walnut Hill*, now called College Hill, on which stand the buildings of Tufts College, partly in Somerville and partly in Medford; and

Strawberry Hill and *Davis Square*, where beauty and art met at the crossroads.

Somerville was first settled in 1630 as a part of Charlestown. At the time of the Revolutionary War, the population was no more than 250, with no more than thirty houses along Cambridge, Winter Hill and Milk Row (Somerville Avenue) roads. Winter, Prospect, Spring, Middle and Walnut Hills were pasturelands, and north of Winter Hill, fields stretched out to the marshes adjacent to the Mystic River.

Separating from Charlestown in 1842, the city was left with few roads, some schoolhouses, a pound and an inadequate fire engine. Not put off by this meager dowry, these early residents were determined to "improve" their rural landscape. Their answer to progress for their community was to build, build, build! Led by the new merchant class and real estate operatives, old farms and estates were divided and sold—subdivided again and again, quickly erasing traces of what went before. Good transportation, coupled with great publicity, encouraged growth, making it one of the most densely populated communities in the nation. Lots of great people. Lots of great stories. Enjoy.

Chapter 1

Ten Hills

BECOMING SETTLED

PEACE FOR LAND

"It is very beautiful in open lands, mixed goodly woods, and again open plains…no place barren but on the tops of the hills. The grass and weeds grow up to a man's face in the lowlands, and by fresh rivers abundance of grass and large meadows. Alewife Brook teemed with fish and the Mystic River was plentifully supplied with smelt."
—*Charlestown Surveyor Thomas Graves, 1630*

For hundreds of years, Native Americans lived and fished along the Mystic River or "Missi-Tuk." Relatively small in size, Mishawum, later part of Charlestown and Somerville, formed the strategic land link between the great rivers of the Mystic and the Charles. Even in this fertile paradise, all did not remain peaceful.

Nanapashemet, the great leader of the Massachuset Federation, ruled over an area stretching from the Blue Hills to the Merrimack River, and from the Atlantic Ocean to the Connecticut River Valley. In 1615, the Mi'Kmag made war on the Penobscot of Maine, killing the chief, his wife and children. Nanapashemet sent a war party in defense of his friends to the north. The war between the tribal nations raged on and was followed by a deadly plague (probably smallpox) that killed almost three-quarters of his tribe. For protection, Nanapashemet moved his wife and children from their home in Salem to the traditional hunting grounds along the Mystic River. Left with too few warriors for his own defense, Nanapashemet was killed in a raid in 1619.

The squa sachem, Nanapashemet's widow, assumed the role of sachem, or chief, until her sons came of age. In 1633, tragedy struck again and her two eldest sons died during another epidemic that decimated the remaining members of the tribe. During the epidemic, some of the colonists took native children into their homes, hoping to save them from death. Mr. John Wilson, pastor of Boston, and even Governor John Winthrop are said to have cared for the squa sachem's own grandsons. Times were changing. The white settlers were coming in increasing numbers and there were continued threats from

A view of Charlestown as seen from Somerville. Gleason's Pictorial Drawing Room Companion, *1854.*
Courtesy of the Somerville Public Library.

hostile tribes to the north and east. The squa sachem had few choices. She made peace with the English—and what they wanted for peace was land.

In 1639, the squa sachem deeded the land in the town of Charlestown, and what is now Somerville, to the English colonists for the sum of twenty-one coats, nineteen fathom of wampum and three bushels of corn. She reserved for herself and her people the west side of the Mystic Pond for hunting and fishing.

Early evidence of the Massachuset people in Somerville is found dating back to the seventeenth century. On May 26, 1631, the squa sachem's sons, Montowampate (Sagamore James) and Wohohaquaham (Sagamore John), complained to Governor John Winthrop that they had been defrauded of twenty beaver pelts by a man in England. The governor entertained them and gave them the name of a lawyer in London, Emanual Downing, Winthrop's brother-in-law. On another occasion that year, Winthrop wrote:

> *The governor, being at his farm house* [Ten Hills] *at Mistick, walked out after supper, and took a piece in his hand, supposing he might see a wolf, for they came daily about the house, and, being about half a mile off, it grew suddenly dark, so as, in coming home, he mistook his path, and went till he came to a little house of Sagamore John, which stood empty. There he stayed, and having a piece of match in his pocket, he made a good fire near the house, and lay down upon some old mats, which he found there, and so spent the night.*

The squa sachem finally submitted to the jurisdiction of the Massachusetts Bay Colony by signing a Treaty of Submission in 1644. She died in 1667. The last remaining members of the Massachuset were removed to Praying Indian Village in Natick and other areas farther inland.

MODEL COMMUNITY

> *A City set upon the hills*
> *For all to see like Ancient Rome,*
> *The one our classic memory thrills,*
> *The other speaks of us of home.*
>
> *It stretches north, and east, and west,*
> *The world is lying at our feet,*
> *Each one believes his view is best,*
> *And makes the harmony complete.*
> *—Martha Perry Lowe, 1892*

John Winthrop and other prominent Puritans organized the Massachusetts Bay Company in 1629 to settle in the New World. Still onboard ship, Winthrop expressed his hopes for the new community in a sermon, "Model of Christian Charity" (1630). Winthrop wrote:

> *We must consider that we shall be as a city upon a hill. The eyes of all people are upon us. So that if we shall deal falsely with our God in this work we have undertaken, and so cause him to withdraw his present help from us, we shall be made a story and a byword throughout the world.*

Following in Winthrop's footsteps, over twenty thousand families settled in New England in the 1630s. Early writings of these settlers sound like real estate advertisements. One early settler wrote, "The sea, the rivers, the woods, the fields are well stocked with abundant fish, fowl, furs; the air and water are the purest; the New England air sweeter than old England's"; and most importantly, the writer concludes, the price is right, "We are all freeholders, the rent day doth not trouble us."

For his own city upon a hill, Governor Winthrop chose six hundred acres on the Mystic River granted to him by royal deed in 1631. Winthrop called his new estate "Ten Hills Farm," due to the ten drumlins or elongated hills on the land. Ten Hills Farm was a wild place, a land of thick forest and abundant wildlife. Animals were numerous, including porcupines, raccoons, deer, bear, moose, wolves and even mountain lions. Winthrop was delighted. He wrote to his wife back in England, "My dear wife, we are here in a paradise."

From his wharf at Ten Hills Farm, Governor Winthrop built and launched the *Blessing of the Bay* on July 4, 1631, considered to be the first ship built by the English in Massachusetts.

Robert Temple House, ca. 1770.

In 1900, several centuries removed from the site of Winthrop's wharf, the Metropolitan Park Commission acquired land in Ten Hills along the Mystic River. A portion of the shore became a popular bathing beach, with a wooden bathhouse built between 1906 and 1908. One older resident recalled, "I remember walking to the beach, passing by the Ford plant and seeing all the workers…we used to swim across the river, right near all of the factories."

Robert's Temple on a Hill

In 1677, the heirs of Governor Winthrop split Ten Hills Farm, deeding 504 acres (in what is now Medford) to Sir Isaac Royal and the remaining 504 acres (in what is now Charlestown and Somerville) to Sir Robert Temple.

At the time, Temple Street was a narrow lane thick with trees leading down from Winter Hill to the Temple House, which is said to have stood very near, if not exactly upon, the site of Winthrop's original farmhouse. The Temple House was very large, with a spacious hall, numerous square rooms and a snug little apartment at the back overlooking the Mystic River. According to some old accounts, Sir Robert Temple had the home designed and erected in England, dismantled and brought to America.

In one of these apartments, there was a dark brown spot, said to be a bloodstain, which no amount of washing could remove. The legend was that a ship, whose commander was part trader and part pirate, was in the habit of mooring his craft at the Ten Hills wharf. The captain was said to have enticed a young girl into the garret and, with the aid of his servant, killed her there. It is said that on stormy nights, her spirit could be seen hovering over the roof or at the windows of the house.

Upon the death of Sir Robert Temple, the property came into the possession of Robert Temple Jr., an infamous royalist. On September 1, 1774, the British sailed up the Mystic River and landed at the Temples' wharf. They marched to the powder house, seizing gunpowder and committing one of the first hostile acts against the colonists. On

June 17, 1775, at the time of the Battle of Bunker Hill, the Continental army made a stand at Ten Hills, but the Americans were forced to retreat. The British established themselves at the Temple House, using the large east-end parlor as a stable for their horses, while the men and officers occupied the rest of the house.

As things were heating up, in May 1755 Robert Temple attempted to return to England. His ship set sail from Boston but sprung a leak and was forced to stop in Plymouth. Temple was taken prisoner and brought to Cambridge Camp. During this time, Temple's family continued to reside at Ten Hills under the protection of Continental General Artemas Ward. While held at Plymouth, on May 31, 1775, Temple addressed a letter to the committee of safety about his troubles back home.

> *I, Robert Temple, of Ten Hills, New-England, do declare, that I have been so threatened, searched for, attacked by the name of tory, an enemy to this Country, and treated in such a manner, that not only my own judgment, but that of my friends, and of almost the whole of the Town where I lived, made it necessary or prudent for me to fly from my home. I am confident that this is owing to the wickedness of a few, very few, who have prejudiced some short-sighted people against me, who live too far from my abode to be acquainted with my proper character.*

Harriet Temple, Robert's wife and the daughter of former Massachusetts Governor William Shirley, pleaded on her husband's behalf to the Continental Congress. She asked that her husband be returned to Boston and that they be granted compensation for damages done to their property, including cutting down trees for firewood and damage to their stables and dairy. After numerous delays, the Temples were paid for the damage done to their farm, and they returned home to Ireland in 1780.

The Sacred Cow of Property

In early times, much of the land in Somerville was known as the "cow commons" or "stinted pasture." Each inhabitant of Charlestown was given a number of "dividends," or areas of land, in order to graze their cattle. At an hour after sunrise, a herdsman would collect the cattle and drive them to the best grazing places. Shares in the commons could be bought, sold or inherited. In his will, Charlestown Deacon Thomas Lynde (1671) bequeathed to his wife "two cow commons near Menotomy [now Somerville], the servant Negros Peter and girl Nan and several building dwellings." He noted that seven of the commons fell to him "in dividend" and he had bought one from James Matthews. All this was about to change.

In 1686, King James II appointed Sir Edmund Andros royal governor of New England. He was now governor of Massachusetts, Rhode Island, Connecticut and New Hampshire, and in 1688 his rule extended over New York and New Jersey. As royal governor, Andros had complete power to make laws and assess taxes, as well as unlimited authority over property. He ruled as a virtual dictator. Andros abolished

The family cow, Marchi family of Derby Street. *Courtesy of Marie Marchi Bonello.*

the representative assembly, limited town meetings and forbade an attempt to start a newspaper in Boston.

Andros declared, "Where ever an Englishman sets his foot, all that he hath is the King's." Andros outraged the citizens of Charlestown, especially those living "beyond the neck" (in Somerville), when he declared that all the property in the stinted pasture would be given to Lieutenant Colonel Charles Lidgett, a follower of Andros and then-owner of Ten Hills Farm. Andros nullified all previous land titles, including some that had been in the same family for over half a century. Colonel Lidgett didn't help matters. He fined and imprisoned former landowners for cutting wood and trespassing on what was previously their own land. The struggle lasted three years.

On April 18, 1689, colonists crossed on the Charlestown ferry to join their Boston brothers in rebellion against the governor. It was written that fifteen hundred more men sought to join the rebellion but were limited by the numbers that could be ferried across the river. Andros and Lidgett were seized and imprisoned at Castle Island in Boston Harbor.

The day after Andros's imprisonment, news arrived in America that King James II of England had been overthrown in what became known as the Glorious Revolution. On April 11, 1689, William III and Mary II (King James's daughter) were crowned as co-rulers of England. Before their coronation, William and Mary accepted the English Bill of Rights, swearing an oath to uphold the laws made by Parliament. The bill is said to have been the inspiration for the American Bill of Rights. Andros was held prisoner in Boston until 1690, when he was sent back to England for trial. In a strange twist of fate, Andros found favor with the new king and was sent back to the colonies as governor of Virginia (1692) and Maryland (1693).

A Crime to Set Them Free

Massachusetts was the first slaveholding colony in New England. Ten Hills Farm was home to five generations of slave owners, including Governor John Winthrop. Winthrop noted in his journal that a ship arrived from Bermuda: "Mr. Pierce, in the Salem ship, the *Desire*, returned from the West Indies after seven months. He brought cotton, and tobacco, and Negroes."

In 1749, the evils of slavery would lead to what would be called "the first great crime in Charlestown." Captain John Codman, a sea captain, was a harsh man and the owner of many slaves whom he employed as mechanics, common laborers and house servants. Three of his most trusted slaves were Mark, Phyllis and Phoebe. After much mistreatment, the servants set fire to their master's workshop, hoping that due to the destruction Codman would be compelled to sell them. The plot failed and their bondage continued.

Six years later, in 1755, the servants once again conspired to gain their freedom, this time by murdering Codman. Some five or six slaves took part in the conspiracy. Mark, who was able to read, claimed the Bible told him he could murder his master without sin if done without bloodshed or by poison. Mark obtained arsenic with the help of Robin, a servant of North End apothecary Dr. William Clark. The two female house servants, Phyllis and Phoebe, made a solution of the poison and added it from time to time to Codman's hot chocolate, which was given innocently to him by his daughter Betty. Codman died on July 1, 1755. Just one day later, the murder was discovered.

Phoebe testified against Mark and Phyllis and was banished to the West Indies. Mark and Phyllis received the ultimate punishment. On September 18, 1755, Middlesex Sheriff Richard Foster issued a warrant of execution for between the hours of one and five o'clock. The two slaves were carted on a sled to the place of execution on the northerly side of Cambridge Road, now Washington Street. Mark was hanged, and Phyllis, an older slave, was burned to death, which was considered to be a less harsh punishment. The body of Mark is said to have remained on the gibbet or hanging cage until a short time before the American Revolution. As Dr. Caleb Rea passed through Charlestown on the first day of June 1758, he found Mark's body. Another Patriot, Paul Revere, in describing his famous ride on April 18, 1775, wrote:

> *I set oft upon a very good horse; It was then about 11 o clock, and very pleasant. After I had passed Charlestown Neck and got nearly opposite where* Mark *was hung- in chains, I saw two men on horseback under a tree.*

Revere's description clearly shows that the site was well known into his time. Slavery was finally abolished in Massachusetts in the 1780s.

Ten Hills Farm was home to five generations of slave owners. Pictured is an early advertisement of a cargo of slaves bound for Charles Town, South Carolina.

COLONEL JACQUES' ARK

According to Edmund Ruffin in *The Farmer's Register* (1840), Ten Hills Farm was one of the most attractive places to the agriculturist in the entire vicinity of Boston. Since 1830, the farm was managed and later owned by Colonel Samuel Jacques and extended from Cross Street to the Medford line between Broadway and the Mystic River.

Colonel Jacques was considered "quaint" and took on the manners of an English country gentleman. He was an ardent horticulturalist and farmer and also kept hounds for hunting fox. Neighbors recalled hearing the call of his bugle and the cry of the pack when Jacques went on the hunt. Jacques occupied Ten Hills for twenty-eight years and entertained many notable dignitaries, including Daniel Webster and Henry Clay.

Colonel Jacques is mostly remembered as an excellent animal breeder. He owned a famous stallion, Bell-Founder, which was the best trotting and running horse in the country. Jacques bred a distinct breed of American dairy cow he named the "cream-pot breed." The cows produced amazing quantities of the richest milk, affording large quantities of butter. Jacques raved that he had a cow that "produced nine pounds of the best butter in three days." At one time, his daughter, Harriett Jacques, made butter before the state legislature and the governor.

Ten Hills was also known for its sheep. For centuries, Spain had closely guarded its renowned merino flocks. These sheep produced high-quality wool that was strong, elastic and took dye well. A single sheep could sell for as high as $1,000. Merchant Ellas Hasket

Merino sheep. *From* Social Life in Old New England, *1914.*

Derby, "America's first millionaire" and a former owner of Ten Hills, brought the sheep to Somerville in 1811. He imported a shipload of eleven hundred merino sheep from Lisbon. These sheep had been driven, illegally, across the mountains from Spain by the French army. They were put on a ship and transported to New York and then to Ten Hills wharf. Soon after, Derby established the first broadcloth loom to manufacture cloth from the merino wool in Massachusetts. Colonel Jacques continued to breed the sheep and is said to have had a prized merino ram that produced forty-two pounds of wool at three shearings.

One of the most interesting visitors to Ten Hills was the pirate Captain Kidd. Captain Kidd, when pursued, hid himself in Sir Robert Temple's smoke room, where the servants cooked hams. This room was entered by means of a trapdoor leading out of a bedroom closet. Captain Kidd may have buried treasure on the land. Later, residents of Ten Hills remember being awakened to the sound of spades and shovels of men who came to dig for the treasure supposedly buried under the house.

Jacques did find treasure in the soil. Besides farming, Colonel Jacques owned a large brickyard on the land that is now Foss (Broadway) Park. Jacques' heirs further reduced the hill for clay pits in the second half of the nineteenth century. Houses were built on the Ten Hills land shortly after World War I. The Temple House was torn down in 1877.

Visiting the Ford Assembly Plant. Ford Somerville News, *February 1954. Courtesy of the Somerville Public Library.*

Like the British soldiers and pirates, later residents also found the Ten Hills location on the Mystic River ideal for transporting goods and people. The area remained a transportation hub into the next century. The construction of the McGrath Highway in 1925 marked the beginning of Somerville as an industrial city. In 1926, the Ford Motor Company built an extensive assembly plant on filled wetlands. Over the next thirty years, Ford would be one of largest employers in the region. In 1957, the plant was retooled for the assembly of the Ford's most elegant and expensive automobile, the Edsel. After a massive promotional campaign, on September 4, 1957, 2.5 million Americans poured into Edsel dealerships on "E-Day." But sales of the Edsel did not meet expectations, and in mid-October 1957, the company ended its production. The Somerville Ford Motor plant closed its doors in 1958, beginning a period of economic decline for the city.

Chapter 2

Cobble Hill
BECOMING PEACEFUL

PUTNAM'S FORTRESS

At Lexington and Concord, on April 19, 1775, the colonists drove the redcoats back to Boston and they were determined to keep them there. In June, Governor Thomas Gage, commander of the British forces, decided to reinforce his defenses by taking Dorchester Heights and occupying Bunker Hill in Charlestown.

In November, General Israel Putnam was ordered to erect a fortification on Cobble Hill in Somerville. As soon as the building began, British ships opened fire upon the troops, but the building continued. A local newspaper described Putnam's fortification at Cobble Hill as "the most perfect…that the American army has constructed during the present campaign," and it was nicknamed "Putnam's Impregnable fortress." It was armed with eighteen and twenty-four pounders and about one thousand men of the Connecticut Line. The Cobble Hill Fort enabled Putnam to fire upon on the British warships on the Charles River and guard the Charlestown Ferry. Low on supplies, the fort may have been less impregnable than it appeared. An eyewitness, surgeon's mate James Thatcher, noted in his diary that "barrels filled with sand and stone were intended to make the position appear more formidable and…if necessary, the rebels would roll the barrels downhill to halt the enemy's advance."

The British continued to bombard the hill, and the Americans repeatedly fired back. The following was written in the diary of Timothy Newell:

> *The man of war of 32 guns which lay opposite kept a constant fire. The first day a shot from Millers Hill took her quarter and went thro' and thro' her—A shot the next day passed my house and struck young Dr. Paddocks hat upon his head, as he was on Dr. [James] Lloyd's hill, the ball fell into his yard. The man of war slipt away in the night.*

The Battle of Bunker Hill began in earnest on June 17, 1775, on Breed's Hill, as part of the larger siege of Boston. The colonists, under General Israel Putnam, repelled two

British attacks before finally retreating as supplies ran low. The British took Breed's and Bunker Hills, but at a great cost, with 800 wounded and 228 killed. Afterward, British General Henry Clinton wrote in his diary, "A few more such victories would have surely put an end to British dominion in America."

A casualty of the battle was the town of Charlestown. Before the war, Charlestown was a town of about three thousand people and about 521 buildings. On the day of the battle, there were only about two hundred citizens still living there. There were also about three hundred members of the colonial militia who used the town as cover to fire upon the British. House-to-house fighting began. The British failed to repel the militia. British commander Baron George Pigot gave the order to set fire to the entire town, both to drive out the remaining Americans and as a show of revenge for British losses at Breed's Hill.

The siege ended when the British sent a message to George Washington. The British declared that if their troops were allowed to leave Boston unchallenged, they would not set fire to the City of Boston. Washington agreed, and the British set sail for Halifax, Nova Scotia, on March 27, 1776. The militia went home, and in April 1776, Washington took most of the forces to New York.

In the summer of 1776, during the Battle of Long Island, George Washington and his troops occupied another Cobble Hill or Coblehill—in New York. The British troops later leveled this hill so that George Washington would not have a strategic vantage point over the British headquarters in Brooklyn Heights.

ON A PLEASANT HILL

With its battles over, Cobble Hill in Somerville would soon become "Pleasant Hill Farm," the peaceful home of former Revolutionary War privateer, smuggler and merchant Joseph Barrell.

Josesph Barrell was born in 1739 to a respected Boston merchant family. A member of the famed Sons of Liberty, Barrell made his fortune as a contractor to the French fleet during the war. As a privateer, Barrell was authorized by the Continental Congress to use his private ships to challenge any likely enemy vessels and disrupt their supply lines.

After the war, Barrell expanded his fortunes further in the fur trade. Inspired by the tales of Captain James Cook and his very profitable Northwest voyages, Barrell entered into a partnership with Dr. Charles Bulfinch; John Derby, a shipmaster; Captain Crowell Hatch of Cambridge; Samuel Brown, a trader of Boston; and John Harden Pintard, a New York merchant. Barrell is said to have remarked, "There is a rich harvest to be reaped by those who are on the ground first out there." The group agreed and purchased two vessels, the *Columbia* and the *Lady Washington*, to travel from New England to the Northwest via China. In August 1790, the *Columbia*, under the command of Captain Robert Gray, returned to Boston, where it received a grand celebration, including a parade up State Street, as the first American vessel to circumnavigate the globe. Barrell wasted no time sending the *Columbia* back to the West Coast. In 1792, Captain Gray

View of McLean Asylum for the Insane, 1853. Note the oncoming train at the left side. The ever-encroaching railroad shattered the peace and quiet of the asylum. Gleason's Pictorial Drawing Room Companion, *1853.*

sailed his ship, the *Columbia*, into the mouth of a great river in Oregon territory, named the river for his vessel and took title to the land for the United States. After receiving a report by Captain Gray, President Thomas Jefferson is said to have sent explorers Lewis and Clark to the territory to explore and expand U.S. claims.

As his businesses expanded, Barrell took on a new employee at his counting house, a young family friend named Charles Bulfinch. A graduate of Boston Latin School and Harvard College, Bulfinch would later become one of America's foremost architects—and the architect of Barrell's new country estate.

In the 1790s, Barrell purchased more than two hundred acres of land on the beautiful Miller's River, a tributary of the Charles. He commissioned Charles Bulfinch to build an impressive mansion, one of Bulfinch's first designs for a private residence. Bulfinch would later go on to build the Massachusetts State House in Boston (1795) and the statehouses in Connecticut (1796) and Maine (1832).

The Barrell Mansion was truly a showplace. The mansion was seventy-four feet long and made of brick. It featured an oval drawing room and a grand and graceful double-flying staircase (now installed at the Somerville Museum). Broad white pine panels, brought from up the Kennebec River, furnished the inside. Barrell is said to have brought some of the granite used in the construction of the house from Scotland on his own ships.

Pleasant Hill Farm was terraced, and water was brought to the top of the hill through a series of driven wheels. Trees and flowers were imported from Europe, as well as the gardeners to care for them. Flights of stone steps led to the beautiful lawns below and ponds filled with gold and silver fish. The land included a two-hundred-foot greenhouse, in which two heating stoves warmed the precious olive, orange and lemon trees that grew inside. In the rear of the house were stables, coach houses and poultry yards. Stately elm and poplar trees bordered the long avenues leading to the grand front door. On the shore stood a boathouse from which Barrell and his guests would travel on an elegant barge, rowed by uniformed oarsmen, down the Miller River to the Charles River and over to Boston.

Joseph Barrell married four times and had twenty children. He is said to have been an original thinker, a good speaker and writer and a lavish entertainer. Among his most famous guests was George Washington when Barrell was chosen to escort the new president from Worcester to Boston.

In 1804, Barrell died suddenly at Pleasant Hill and the land passed to his son-in-law, Benjamin Joy, and daughter, Hannah. In 1816, the trustees of Massachusetts General Hospital bought the estate for a mere $15,650 to establish an asylum for the insane. The Barrell Mansion house would become the residence of the superintendent and other physicians of the hospital.

COMMITMENT TO HIS CARE

Every now and again a community is fortunate enough to attract someone who is so committed to the public good that he becomes the stuff of legend. Such an icon was Dr. Luther V. Bell (1806–62), nationally recognized as the progressive and humane director of McLean Asylum from 1837 to 1855. His efforts in guiding the first school committee in Somerville were equally admired by the newly organized town in 1844. Looking back on the contribution of Bell to the educational interests of his fellow residents, Albert E. Winship, in 1896, enthused:

> *Bell was the most eminent physician, and the most influential man of affairs the city has ever produced. He occupied a prominent place among the educational celebrities of the State.*

Dr. Bell came from an illustrious New Hampshire line. His immediate family considered public service a personal duty through careers in medicine, the law or politics. When he was thirteen, he entered Bowdoin College, where he quickly became close friends with fellow students Nathaniel Hawthorne and Henry Wadsworth Longfellow. After completing a medical degree in New York, he returned to New Hampshire, where he decided to live his life as a country doctor.

Fate intervened in several dramatic events. The first incident involved an intemperate, elderly farmer, whose leg had been crushed by the rolling weight of a heavy country wagon. Since time was critical and amputation of the leg a necessity, Bell improvised by using the patient's razor, an antique saw and a darning needle to perform the operation.

Dr. Luther V. Bell, the forward-thinking superintendent of McLean Asylum for the Insane. Memoir of Luther V. Bell, MD, LLD, *1863.*

Later, the fully recovered farmer was presented with a wooden leg carved by the resourceful young doctor. Dr. Bell was on his way to becoming a local legend.

The next events revolved around what would become his life's work. Several enlightened New Hampshire leaders determined that a special hospital for the treatment of the insane was needed in the state. Bell endorsed the project despite much public opposition. Understanding that the citizens needed to be educated, Bell was elected to the state legislature in order to put all his influence on this pressing problem. He was made chairman of a committee to study the question of establishing the hospital and wrote such a compelling report on the matter that his reputation spread to neighboring Massachusetts and the trustees of Massachusetts General Hospital.

Somerville Hospital, ca. 1894. *Courtesy of Maynard and Laverne Batchelder.*

When Dr. Bell was invited to superintend McLean Asylum, the institution had already been in existence for nineteen years, and upon his arrival it housed seventy patients. The trustees had searched for a director who was fearless, calm and had a great sense of duty coupled with good judgment. Bell was certainly qualified, yet it was his innate power of observation that brought the hospital to an entirely new level. Like a true scientist, Bell knew that he needed to test his theories by involving the trustees and his staff in reviewing his findings. A friend remarked, "He found more to question, to doubt about, and to subject to rigid examination than he did to approve or blindly follow."

The science of treating mental illness was in its infancy, struggling against public indifference and a sense of hopelessness that any great good could be accomplished. Bell developed guidelines that confounded conventional wisdom. He insisted that each patient must be treated as an individual whose abilities and character had to be taken into consideration. Bell urged the staff to channel the residents into individually productive activities. Physical restraints were discontinued whenever possible. Patients could go on staff-chaperoned field trips outside the grounds, providing that they did not become disoriented. During his career, he treated over two thousand men and women with 62 percent enjoying partial or full recovery.

McLean Asylum terrace and walk with view of North Packing Plant, ca. 1885. *Courtesy of Historic New England.*

Living on the asylum grounds, Bell, his wife Frances and their seven children interacted with staff and patients. Another correspondent wrote that Bell "enjoyed very many of the attractions of the private home in the center of a wide circle of patients and professional assistants." Frequent visitors, the trustees offered their loyalty and encouragement. Bell was so grateful to one that he named a son, William Appleton, in the man's honor. Born at McLean in 1851, William Appleton Bell followed his father's calling and studied medicine. A resident of Bow Street, the younger doctor was a member of the Somerville Hospital medical team from its very beginning.

In addition to being an "expert witness" in civil and criminal trials when the defendant appeared to be suffering from a mental disorder, Bell also managed to devote several years to Somerville's first school committee. Again, he applied his considerable influence to erecting schools, determining the policy of the school board and inspiring local teachers with an appreciation of their profession and pupils with a sense of purpose. During his term, 1843–47, he instilled in the town officers the concept that education was the true preparation for responsible citizenship. It was fitting that a school would be named in his honor.

Although the site of the hospital was unsurpassed for healthfulness and beauty, McLean Asylum was faced with a situation beyond Bell's control. Numerous railroad crossings began to encroach upon the hospital grounds. Bell had given such thought to the tranquility of the surroundings that he was astounded that an outside force was threatening to destroy the work of years. He lamented:

> *The almost constant shriek of the steam whistle was a sound certainly not favorable to jarred nerves and morbid sensibilities. Will so much benevolent and scientific outlay* [be sacrificed] *to the conveniences of engineering?*

He had hoped that the roadbeds of the railroads would have been constructed farther away from the grounds of the institution, but that was not the case. Technology trumped health.

Suffering from a heart condition, Bell resigned from McLean in 1855. He had already experienced the loss of his beloved wife, Frances, and the untimely deaths of three of his children. Moving to Monument Square in Charlestown, the serious, pensive Bell was often seen in the garden of his new home, his remaining children helping him to care for the flowers. His thoughts were never far from his hospital.

> *Having made my arrangements to retire to a spot not far distant, where I shall have the happiness of opening my eyes each morning on this blessed institution, and feeling that my own happiness will be intimately connected with its continued prosperity, I hope hereafter to be no stranger within its walls...I will only say that I leave this Asylum prosperous in its own affairs, and amply possessed of the confidence of the community.*

At the onset of the Civil War, Bell offered his medical services to the commonwealth. Although he was in his fifties and past the acceptable age, he was assigned a position as surgeon in the Eleventh Massachusetts Regiment. He wrote home to his children many detailed letters, which he illustrated with lively drawings, longing for the day when he could rejoin them. At the Battle of Bull Run in 1862, he remained with the wounded soldiers who had fallen. Completely exhausted, his heart could not withstand the exertion, and he died within a few days from exposure and fatigue. When Somerville received the news, the many men and women who had benefited from his enlightened views mourned the death of a great friend.

After Bell's passing, McLean continued to be a place of refuge for those with mental illness. McLean would gain a reputation for the writers and artists that spent time at the institution. Ralph Waldo Emerson made frequent visits to the asylum (and often complained of the costs), visiting his brothers Edward and Robert, who were both patients. Emerson's brother-in-law, Boston dentist Charles T. Jackson (who once worked at the McLean Asylum), was also a patient, and he died at the asylum in 1873. Jackson was involved in several patent controversies, including his claim that Thomas Morton had stolen his discovery of ether and Samuel B. Morse had stolen his idea for the telegraph. Jackson's claim of inventing ether was backed by none other than the humorist Mark Twain. Other famous artists and writers who were patients at McLean include Sylvia

An 1874 Sanborn map of McLean Asylum showing the proposed house lots. Few homes were ever built.

Plath (*The Bell Jar*), Susanna Kaysen (*Girl, Interrupted*), musician Ray Charles and John Forbes Nash (*A Beautiful Mind*).

McLean Asylum in Somerville also came to a fateful end. Gradually, the railroads, slaughterhouses and rendering plants surrounded Cobble Hill and it soon became necessary to relocate the asylum. Somerville resident Columbus Tyler testified in a court case by the State Board of Health against the John P. Squire's (meatpacking) Company for engaging in "noxious or offensive trades." McLean Asylum relocated to Belmont in 1895. The Cobble Hill property was sold to the Boston and Maine Railroad for $500,000. The railway company tore down sixteen structures, nearly all built of stone and brick, including the former Barrell Mansion. It cut down fifteen hundred elm and maple trees and uprooted hundreds of fruit trees and rosebushes, making way for the growing rail yards.

By the early 1900s, there were several proposals to connect Somerville to the communities to the west and north of the city. In the 1950s, most of the historical homes in Brickbottom were demolished in anticipation of the construction of the Inner Belt Expressway and the redevelopment of the Inner Belt Industrial Park. In the late 1980s, the Brickbottom area would once again see residential development.

Eighty-five artists purchased the A&P food-storage warehouse located at the corner of McGrath Highway and Fitchburg Street and established the Brickbottom Artists Cooperative.

Mary Sawyer's Little Lamb

> *Mary had a little lamb,*
> *Its fleece was white as snow;*
> *And everywhere that Mary went,*
> *The lamb was sure to go.*
> *He followed her to school one day;*
> *That was against the rule;*
> *It made the children laugh and play;*
> *To see a lamb at school.*
>
> *And so the teacher turned it out,*
> *But still it lingered near,*
> *And waited patiently about*
> *Till Mary did appear.*
> *"Why does the lamb love Mary so?"*
> *The eager children cry;*
> *"Why, Mary loves the lamb, you know,"*
> *The teacher did reply.*

Somerville is rich in history. Many great men and women have walked its streets. But no poet, artist or politician is as famous worldwide as Somerville's Mary (Sawyer) Tyler. Most readers are familiar with the story of Mary and her fondness for a certain little lamb, but most do not know that there really was a Mary—and there really was a lamb—and that Mary lived in Somerville.

In the 1880s, Mary and her lamb were so famous that Bishop John Hamilton of the Methodist Episcopal Church said, "I have to tell the story of Mary and her lamb more frequently than I am asked to talk about Emerson or any one of several great men of our nation whom I knew there." So famous was the poem that Thomas Edison reported that "Mary had a Little Lamb" were the first words ever recorded and played back on a phonograph.

Mary Elizabeth Sawyer was born on a farm in the small village of Sterling in 1806. In 1827, Mary secured a position at the McLean Asylum for the Insane, where she remained as matron for thirty-five years. In 1835, she married Columbus Tyler. Born in Vermont, Columbus Tyler moved to Somerville to take a position as an attendant at the asylum. He worked his way up to steward and then to general superintendent. He was greatly esteemed for his work with the mentally ill and his assistance to men such as Dr. Luther V. Bell.

Mary Sawyer Tyler
at thirty-five years
of age. The Story of
Mary's Little Lamb,
1928.

After leaving the asylum, the Tylers built a spacious home on Central Street, now the site of the Greek Orthodox Church. Columbus was active in the movement to set off Somerville from Charlestown and was later a representative to the state legislature. Mary and Columbus were founding members of the First Unitarian Church. Mary, known by her friends as "Aunt Mary," was active in the Women's Christian Temperance Union and the Women's Relief Corps and was one of the founders of the Women's Industrial Exchange. Although they had no children of their own, their love of children was evident. In his will, Columbus bequeathed their home and grounds to the Unitarian Society, with stipulations that children (with their attendants) were to have free access to the grounds. A fund was also set up to provide an annual stipend for any child who regularly attended Sunday school.

Columbus and Mary Tyler's estate on Central Street.

In her later years, Mrs. Tyler became involved in preservation causes. At eighty years old, she was asked to donate the stockings her mother had knit from the fleece of the famed lamb for the preservation of the Old South Meetinghouse. One of the stockings was unraveled and sold in small bits, tied to a card bearing Mary's autograph. When all the yarn had sold, the Boston ladies wanted more. Mary, without hesitation, donated the other stocking and kept for herself only two small cards with just bits of yarn. It was said that the donation raised $200.

But what of the story of Mary's lamb? Mary Sawyer is said to have told the story, with very little variation, many times to her neighbors, visiting newspaper reporters and countless fascinated children. According to Mary, it all began one cold March day when Mary, accompanying her father, found a tiny baby lamb near death in the barn.

> *I used to take as much care of my pet lamb as a mother would of a child; used to wash it regularly, keep the burdocks out of its wool, comb and trim with bright-colored ribbons the wool on its forehead; and when that was being done the lamb would hold down its head, shut its eyes and stand patiently as could be. I was always very fond of animals, and from the time I could toddle out to the barn I was with the dumb beasts not a little of the time. My brother Nat said, Let's take the lamb to school with us. I thought it would be a good idea and I consented, and she followed right along behind me. Well, I put the lamb under the seat, put on her blanket, and she lay down just as quietly as could be. By*

and by I had to go out to recite and left the lamb all right, but in a moment there was a clatter, and I knew it was the pattering hoofs of my lamb. O! How mortified I felt. The teacher laughed outright, and of course all the children giggled. It was rare sport for them, but I couldn't find anything mirthful about the situation. I took the lamb and put it in a shed until I was ready to go home at noon, when it followed me back.

Visiting the school that forenoon was a local minister's nephew, John Roulstone (1805–22). Roulstone was so pleased with Mary and her young lamb that he came back the next day and handed Mary a slip of paper containing the original twelve lines of the now-famous poem.

The poem "Mary Had a Little Lamb" was first published in 1830 in a booklet entitled *Poems for Our Children* by Mrs. Sarah J. Hale. Hale was the editor of *Godey's Lady's Book* from 1837 to 1877, and the author of twenty books and hundreds of poems. Hale insisted that the poem was her own and was not based on any actual event. She said of Mary's story, "There may have been other lambs anxious for an education who braved the New England schoolmarm, but the one in [my] poem existed only in [my] imagination." In the 1830s, Lowell Mason set the nursery rhyme to a melody written by Mozart, adding repetition in the verses.

Columbus and Mary Tyler lived happily ever after in their elegant home until their deaths in 1881 and 1889. But what of Mary's lamb? Mary told the story in a book published by Henry Ford (the carmaker) entitled *The Story of Mary's Little Lamb As Told By Mary and Her Neighbors and Friends.*

I have not told you about the death of my little playmate. It occurred on a Thanksgiving morning. We were all out in the barn, where the lamb had followed me. It ran right in front of the cows. One of the creatures gave its head a toss, then lowered is horns and gored my lamb, which gave a piercing, agonizing bleat, and came toward me with the blood streaming from its side. I took it in my arms, placed its head in my lap, and there it bled to death. It was a sorrowful moment for me, for the companion of many of my romps, my playfellow of many a long summer's day, had given up its life, and its place could not be filled in the childish heart.

Chapter 3

Ploughed Hill
BECOMING OPEN-MINDED

INDEPENDENCE UNDER FIRE

Sixty years before the Mount Benedict outrage, bands of sturdy citizen soldiers had pulled cannons up the side of Ploughed Hill in order to protect Charlestown. The objective was to confine the British within the limits of Boston. These undisciplined yet determined men quickly covered the summit of the hill with fortifications. The earthworks were within thirteen hundred yards of the British stationed on Bunker Hill, providing each side with a clear sight of the opponent. Sheltered by their entrenchments, troops primarily from New Hampshire and Rhode Island hunkered down to outlast an enemy who had fired over three hundred shells at them in just a few day. The strategy was unglamorous but effective. During their months on Ploughed Hill, the soldiers were united by their common resolve. Their location tested their endurance in the face of constant shelling from the equally determined British. After the Revolution, souvenir hunters would explore the remains of the fortifications in the hope of finding cannonballs or musket shot. No one anticipated that the site would become known for a tragedy centered on intolerance.

A SPARK OF EDUCATION

At the very beginning of the nineteenth century, the Boston congregation of Catholics had grown from 100 parishioners to 1,250. They prospered amid their Protestant countrymen, so much so that Charles Bulfinch designed the Catholic cathedral on Franklin Street. After a few years passed, Bishop Fenwick, then in charge, purchased the lot of land next to the church with the intent of establishing a school for the instruction of young women. Staffed by sisters from the Order of Saint Ursula, it was fabulously successful and soon outgrew Franklin Street. The academy was a testament to the hard work of the Ursulines, who in six short years (1820–26) had brought their school into such prominence that it was honored by many Protestants and most Catholics. The new facility was to be located on Ploughed Hill on the remains of the old Revolutionary fortifications. During construction, the sisters and their charges occupied the Charlestown farmhouse of Arnold Cook. They eagerly awaited their new accommodations.

The results were elegant and rather elaborate. By the 1830s, the landscape of Ploughed Hill, now christened Mount Benedict in honor of the sisters' benefactor, had been transformed from nothing remarkable to a place of tasteful gardens filled with flowers and berry bushes. The large school building was three stories high, red bricked and had wings that embraced an inner courtyard. It was highly visible to the men working in the brickyards at the foot of the hill. Breezes from the Mystic River drifted near the fiery kilns and up the hill to the secluded terraces. The nearby Middlesex Canal carried heavily laden barges back and forth from Boston to the towns of the interior, finally ending in Lowell. It was a scene of earnest productivity.

The schoolgirls enjoyed an ambitious curriculum. Philosophy, various types of drawing, geometry, botany, arithmetic, needlework, music, cooking and rhetoric were some of the courses offered. One of the former pupils wrote an open letter to the *Boston Transcript* in 1843 wherein she offered her view of the elite academy. She recalled that the school was divided into senior and junior classes, each having its own set of teachers. She reminisced:

> *In summer time we often took our work and sat under the trees while one of the young ladies read to us. Sometimes the Nuns would invent stories for our amusement…Punishments of any sort were very rare.*

The student body was composed almost entirely of upper-class Protestant girls. The above quoted writer, herself a Protestant, described the environment.

> *In religious matters we were never interfered with….No difference was ever to be observed in the conduct of the Sisters towards their pupils. All shared alike in their care and kindnesses. The number of [Catholics] was very small, never exceeding ten or twelve and usually not more than half that number, while the Protestant pupils averaged, I should think, nearly forty.*

In 1834, Anna Augusta Parkman was thirteen and had been attending the Mount Benedict academy for several months. Born into a Protestant family of wealth and social prominence, she was happy to be a Unitarian and attend services in Boston's King's Chapel. Her family's farm in rural Brighton prepared her for the gardens and orchards of the boarding school. Her father, the Reverend John Parkman, loved being a country gentleman and minister. Anna's lifestyle was sheltered, comfortable and perfect for a young girl who could profit from the Ursulines' sophisticated teaching. Despite the simplicity of the school dress code, Anna managed to personalize her appearance. One of her friends, Louisa Goddard Whitney, described her with great admiration:

> *One little girl wore a superb [hair] net with lovely tassels, all blue saddler's silk. "Too lovely for anything!," I thought, both her and her net…The little girl was called Anna Augusta; such an appropriate name, I [mused], for the owner of that exquisite thing.*

Anna was completely unprepared for the outrage that descended upon her secure and beautiful world during the summer of what would be her last year at school.

In the Heat of the Moment

In August 1834 rumors of forced conversions to Catholicism, a nun being held against her will and other juicy suppositions were flying about Charlestown. They had been foreshadowed by the story of Rebecca Reed, who had been a student of and then a candidate for the Ursuline community. Her brief time at Mount Benedict was later published under the title of *Six Months in a Convent*, but the sensational events she described were already part of town gossip and contributing to the anti-Catholic sentiments. Because there was "an excited state of feelings among the people," many wondered not if, but when, everything would boil over.

The event began rather quietly. Public notices were posted in Charlestown threatening the very existence of Mount Benedict. Alarmed, the selectmen, wanting

The ruins of the Ursuline Convent at Charlestown. The walls and chimneys are still remaining soon after the riot of August 11, 1834. *Original engraving from the* Cyclopedia of Useful Knowledge, *1834–1835.*

to prevent trouble, toured the premises but found nothing questionable. They were escorted through the complex by Miss Harrison, also known as Sister Mary John, who had fallen into a hysterical fit several weeks earlier and run from the convent, only to be returned a day later with a much calmer outlook. More rumors had it that she was being held against her will. Other stories circulated that she had been imprisoned and might even have been murdered. Although the Charlestown selectmen had assured the mother superior that there was no cause for alarm, they had greatly underestimated the volatility of the situation.

On Monday night, the eleventh, a quarrelsome mob, some with painted faces, gathered at the gates and demanded to see Sister Mary John. The mother superior refused to produce the frightened sister and ordered the crowd of about a hundred angry and drunken Protestants to disperse. She quoted the selectmen as having absolved the convent of any misconduct. With their fury mounting, the rioters realized that the students and sisters were unprotected. To the girls who were huddled in the corridor, the crowd appeared "like a dense black mass…whose voices were like the yells of fiends."

For a brief time, the mob retreated to a bonfire burning near the school. Individuals began offering emotional diatribes to stimulate the crowd even more. One of the company brandished a club, beat down the convent door and led the surge into the building. Quickly gathering up the fifty or more girls, the sisters and their pupils sought sanctuary near the mausoleum, the burial place for deceased nuns. The mob approached. The quick-thinking mother superior led her charges through an adjacent field and down the hill to safety. Many of the girls suffered bruises from their traumatic flight over the rough ground. Neighbors, such as John C. Magoun on Winter Hill, offered the shaken victims a place of refuge.

When the rioters stormed the building, their fury increased. Furniture, pianos, harps, the chapel altar and sacred items were thrown into the flames. Bishop Fenwick's lodge, library, the school stables and outbuildings were engulfed. The dresses and personal mementos of the students were confiscated and burned. Most troubling was the desecration of the convent tomb. The coffins were ripped open and the bones scattered and trampled.

On the night of the convent disaster, firefighters from the Boston area responded to the alarms raised by the sight of flames leaping into the sky. Years later, two eyewitness accounts reported what the men faced. One resident, speaking on the condition of anonymity, recollected the sequence of events in a *Globe* article of the 1890s. He said that when the mob rushed onto the grounds, they torched the tar barrels that had been thrown against the school walls. The emboldened looters flung firebrands through broken windows just as firemen from Charlestown and Cambridge arrived on the scene. Intimidated by the crowd's fury, the fire companies backed down from any effort to control the blaze. Meanwhile, the Boston firefighters pulled up and, taking their cue from their colleagues, remained passive.

The second witness, just a boy at the time of the tragedy, recollected that he had often visited the grounds at the invitation of Bishop Fenwick. When the old Mystic No. 6 arrived, George W. Fillebrown said that he ran to meet the volunteers and directed them

Ruin of the Ursuline Convent, ca. 1850s. Gleason's Pictorial Drawing Room Companion. *Courtesy of the Somerville Public Library.*

to the family well, but not surprisingly, the bucket brigade proved completely ineffective. Soon, all Fillebrown and the Mystic firefighters could do was watch the flames devour the property.

The next day, the twelfth, the Boston press condemned the outrage and mass meetings were held in Faneuil Hall, Charlestown and Cambridge. But the violence was not yet quelled. A smaller mob marched on the Franklin Street Church but did not harm it. They continued on to Charlestown, where they lit a large bonfire, using the convent fences as fuel. Then they returned to Mount Benedict to destroy the terraced gardens, the fruit trees and anything else still standing. Now completely alarmed, officials in Boston called out the military, groups of concerned citizens formed armed patrols and a vigilance committee was assembled. Calmer voices began to prevail as Bishop Fenwick and leading Protestants of the area urged nonviolence. Gradually, the fever abated.

Both city and state offered rewards for the apprehension and conviction of the ringleaders. About a dozen men stood trial, but nothing substantial came of it. There was a generous amount of blame handed out. Charlestown selectmen were seen as incompetent, while they, in turn, accused Boston of allowing unsavory individuals to assemble in Charlestown. Meanwhile, Bishop Fenwick asked for compensation; however, he met with strong opposition. Requests for money were put forth every few years until 1854. There was never any resolution. The ruins remained undisturbed, bearing mute testimony to a night of destruction and violence.

COMING TO A COMMON GROUND

The Mount Benedict property was sold to a syndicate of wealthy gentlemen who attempted to reclaim the nunnery grounds. In the early 1870s, they envisioned a prime residential area being created out of the abandoned hilltop and other land located on Broadway. The investors included George O. Brastow and Clark Bennett, a firefighter and member of the first town council. Initially, the project began with great gusto. Some of the hilltop was scraped off in order to fill in a portion of the old clay pits skirting the perimeter of the hill. A couple of streets were laid out and some modest houses began to dot the landscape.

The jewel in the crown, however, depended on the widening of Broadway and the creation of a large public park. The land in question encompassed sixteen marshy acres between Mount Benedict and Winter Hill. It formed a natural basin nesting in the middle of the two elevations and was fast becoming a public health nuisance. Owners of adjacent estates on Broadway—such as Seman Klous, an investor and chief proponent of the park—wanted something to be done as soon as possible. The best idea, he reasoned, would be to have the city purchase the acreage, improve it and dedicate it to public use. After much debate, officials voted to spend $200,000 and name the venture a Great Public Improvement.

Contracts for filling the land were awarded, trees were purchased and curbing was supplied for a man-made pond that would be the park's centerpiece. In an article entitled "Inland Navigation," the *Somerville Journal* enthused that the pond would be shallow enough for children to play in, yet deep enough for the rowboats that could be rented by the hour. "The boats are staunch, and all the way from eight to fourteen foot keel—big enough for a couple of lovers, or for a moderately sized family party."

With such ambitious plans afoot, there were enormous cost overruns, insinuations of padding of hours by city workers and accusations of mishandling of public moneys. The rumor mill again was activated, but this time it was fueled by a different source. Instead of using religion as a target, angry residents attacked government as the reason for their discontent.

By the next city election, the outcry was so widespread that several of the officials who supported the land purchase were thrown out and an anti-park administration was ushered in. The new team proposed eliminating the park and laying out the area in tax-producing house lots. Surprisingly, they were unsuccessful in derailing Broadway Park. Over time, what had been seen as a folly became an oasis for East Somerville. In 1907, the *Journal* even praised the wise forethought of the city fathers who had created a "blessed spot" in place of the old Happy Hollow, as the former marsh had been called.

Betterment of the rest of the Ploughed Hill area was slow in coming. The leveling of the hill crawled to a stop until 1897, when it was finally made available for building purposes. By the mid-twentieth century, the neighborhood was still coined the "Nunnery Grounds."

SOMERVILLE, MASS. SOMERVILLE PARK.

Postcard, Broadway Park, now Saxton Foss Park, ca. 1910. The park was the cause of great controversy during its construction.

"PLOUGHED HILL"
FORTIFIED AND BOMBARDED
IN 1775-76
SITE OF URSULINE CONVENT
FOUNDED 1820 AND OPENED 1826
BURNED 1834
HILL DUG DOWN 1875 TO 1897

ERECTED BY
MT. BENEDICT COUNCIL No. 75

The Broadway monument marking Ploughed Hill and the site of the Ursuline Convent. The East Branch of the Somerville Public Library is in the background. Photograph 2008.

ALWAYS AT THE READY

The territory that became Somerville was considered the rural section of Charlestown. Firefighting resources were almost nonexistent. Outfitted with buckets, one small hand tub, which was three feet long and two feet wide, was the only official engine available to the all-volunteer fire force. The tank with wheels was given the name of the Mystic No. 6. It was inadequate to fight any serious conflagration, especially the one in 1834.

Within a few years and after several repairs, Mystic No. 6 was scrapped and a state-of-the-art engine was ordered. Costing over $1,000, Somerville No. 1 joined a fifty-five-member firefighting association that had adopted the motto of "Faithful and Fearless." By 1850, Nathan Tufts was appointed the chief engineer, with George O. Brastow as the first clerk.

Gone were the days when every house was required to have two buckets at the ready so that when the alarm sounded the volunteer firemen could have assistance from every adult male. Depending on the town to provide water for firefighting was out of the question. Instead, the department had to rely on private wells or on the reservoirs that had been placed at strategic locations under main roads. Nothing more than large troughs, the reservoirs captured the rain running off streets and buildings. By the 1860s, pipes were being incorporated into street infrastructure with the water supply coming from the Cambridge Water Works or the reservoir on Walnut Hill.

During the Civil War years, almost half the men of the fire company volunteered to serve, thus leaving the town vulnerable and unprotected. Amateur arsonists were provided with an unprecedented opportunity. Every few days, a fire of suspicious origin would sweep through a home or business, leaving the understaffed fire department to cope with not only the blaze, but also the eager yet inexperienced young men who were volunteering to help.

The volunteer system disappeared after 1866, when firemen began to receive a salary from the town. Steam fire engines, hook and ladder carriages, hose carriages and much better equipment in general replaced the hand engines. Alarm boxes were installed at key locations. Increased availability of water, including the setting out of hydrants, eliminated the need for the street reservoirs.

One of Somerville's most illustrious fire chiefs, James R. Hopkins, was born in East Cambridge in 1836, two years after the convent burning. As a young man, he became involved in the furniture-carving trade and honed his skills with a full course in drawing at the Lowell Institute. But his first love had always been the fire department. When he was barely a teenager, Hopkins served as a volunteer and then was elected a member of East Cambridge's Niagara Hand Engine No. 3. Upon removing to Somerville, he quickly joined Hand Engine No. 1 and began moving up the ranks. He was elected chief in 1872.

His abilities were soon tested in November of the same year, when the great fire almost destroyed most of what is now Boston's financial district. Over sixty acres were leveled, including the former site of the first Catholic cathedral on the corner of Franklin Street. Under Hopkins's leadership, the Somerville Fire Department performed heroically.

James R. Hopkins, chief of the fire department for over thirty years.

Even in Hopkins's day, Somerville was a city of wooden homes. Fire-prone industries were located within residential neighborhoods because no one had thought to do otherwise. Frequent, all-consuming blazes were a constant threat in tightly packed blocks where houses, grain depots, stables, blacksmith shops and factories coexisted. In

49

particular, the two pork-rendering plants in East Somerville, the Union Glass Company and other factories manufacturing flammable products posed imminent dangers. To the credit of Hopkins's highly disciplined men and their steam engines, fires were often limited to the burning structures themselves.

Proud to be a Civil War veteran, a musician and an inventor, Hopkins was proactive in all aspects of his job. He lobbied to have all the wards of Somerville given equal fire protection by having well-equipped firehouses in every section of the city. He wrote essays about fire prevention and developed new apparatus that would protect the men who were risking their lives. His design for a metal fire hat became standard issue in Somerville and other cities.

Known as "Uncle Jimmie" to his fire lads, Hopkins found time to be a charter member of the National Association of Fire Engineers, work on a plan for a sharing of Greater Boston Fire Department resources and sing weekly in church choirs of Somerville, Roxbury and Boston. Well into his seventies, he served Somerville with distinction, compassion and an instinctive executive ability. The *Somerville Journal* gave him high praise when it reported that Hopkins was "precise and strict in the control of his department, and as cool and fearless a fireman as ever won the name."

SANBORN'S FIRE MAPS

Daniel A. Sanborn (1827–83), a talented surveyor with a keen eye for business, was a native son of Somerville. As a young man, he was influenced by Charles Elliot, chief engineer of the town and a history buff. Sanborn's considerable drafting skills came to the attention of the Aetna Insurance Company at the end of the Civil War, when the country was on the verge of unprecedented urbanization. Something had to be done to chart the haphazard building boom. Sanborn was the perfect man to do the job.

In 1866, factories were crowding into densely populated neighborhoods. As the use of volatile materials such as kerosene, oil and gas became rampant, the highly flammable buildings posed an ongoing threat to life and property. Narrow, congested streets compounded the problem as local fire departments struggled to quell the increasing number of blazes that devastated whole city blocks. Sanborn's meticulous maps of Boston (and some areas of Tennessee) contained all the necessary details needed to evaluate risk. His work was stellar, providing information as to building use and materials, as well as locations of tanks and measurements of streets.

Soon, Sanborn was on his own, and by 1867 he had founded his own business, the D.A. Sanborn National Insurance Diagram Bureau. Drawn to a scale of fifty feet to one inch, the Sanborn maps filled large sheets with accurate details of urban districts. Today, the company is still providing maps for environmental and insurance professionals.

Chapter 4

Middle Hill

BECOMING PROUD

WHAT'S IN A NAME—WALFORD, MASSACHUSETTS

In November 1841, a meeting was held at the old Prospect Hill schoolhouse to consider the question of separating from Charlestown. There had long been talk among the residents of "the Neck" of perhaps joining Cambridge, Arlington or even Boston. As early as 1828, a petition was presented to the legislature asking that a new town be formed and called Warren, after Bunker Hill martyr General Joseph Warren. This petition was later withdrawn. At the November meeting moderated by Columbus Tyler, the discussion once again turned to forming a new town. Certainly, the residents thought a new town government could provide better services for lower taxes. On March 3, 1842, the governor approved the act of separation.

Now the town just needed a name. On March 3, 1842, a vote was taken and a name was chosen—Walford, in honor of the first white settler. So, for a short time, the matter was resolved, and the citizens of Walford got busy organizing their new town. But it appears, though no records exist, that prominent resident Charles Miller was not fully satisfied with the new name. Miller invited some friends and neighbors to his home to talk the matter over. Miller's arguments were convincing, and on December 13, 1842, the committee voted to change the name to Somerville.

Why did Charles Miller choose "Somerville"? Through the years, many attempts have been made to associate the name with some noted person or place. The Somerville Historical Society concluded in a lengthy report that it was a "purely fanciful name." We may never know why a new name was chosen. But perhaps Charles Miller knew the real story of the Walfords.

When the Puritan settlers arrived in Charlestown in 1629, they reported finding but "one English pallasades [sic] and thatched house, wherein lived Thomas Walford, a smith." Walford and his wife Jane arrived under the charter of Sir Robert Gorges in 1623. Sir Gorges, an Anglican, established a settlement, which failed. Most of the settlers returned to England, "some out of discontent and dislike of the country, others

Somerville City Hall with its old entrance fronting Highland Avenue, formerly the Old Somerville High School.

Early seal of the City of Somerville.

by reason of a fire that broke out and burnt the houses they lived in and all their provisions." The Walfords stayed on—until they were forced out.

As the Massachusetts Bay Colony grew, trouble began for those deemed "unsympathetic" to the Puritans. In May 1631, the general court ordered that "Walford depart out of the limits of this patent before the 20th day of October next, under pain of confiscation of his goods, for his contempt of authority & confronting officers" or more so for his "Anglican tenets." The Walfords defied authorities until 1635, when they relocated to Strawberry Banke, now part of Portsmouth.

In their new home, the Walfords continued to battle their neighbors over land and religion. Due to land disputes, Jane Walford was accused of being a witch in 1648, 1656 and 1669. Although there are no records of Jane being accused of witchcraft in Charlestown, the practice did exist. In his journal, Governor Winthrop wrote that in June 1648, Margaret Jones of Charlestown was indicted and found guilty of witchcraft and hanged for it.

In the case of Jane Walford, it was her neighbors who testified against her. Neighbor Susannah Trimmings deposed on April 18, 1656:

> *There did appear to her a woman whom she apprehended to by old Goodwife Walford. She asked me where my consort was; I answered I had none. She said lend me a pound of cotton. I told her I had but two pounds in the house, and I would not spare any to my mother…She then left me, and I was struck as with a clap of fire on the back, and she vanished toward the water side, in my apprehension in the shape of a cat.*

Jane repeatedly took on her accusers and won, and she was never found guilty of any charges. Despite their troubles, the Walford family prospered and became wealthy landowners. However, the stigma of witch passed to Jane's five daughters, including Hannah Jones, who was accused of witchcraft in 1681.

THE PLEASANT POLITICIAN

George O. Brastow knew how to get things done. His strong common sense plus his hearty and jovial manner cut through the difficulties inherent in creating a functioning town. Another enormously useful quality was his ability to develop a personal rapport with every individual he met. His name was identified with the development of Somerville because he was engaged in almost every enterprise that was started for the welfare of the community.

Born in Wrentham, George Brastow came to Charlestown in 1838 without any clear mission, except buying land and building houses. One of the earliest subdivisions, a year after Somerville was made independent, was his mapping out of land on Spring Hill's southern slope. He was indeed a speculator, but with the difference that he wanted to preserve the character of the town. He promoted the interests of Somerville by serving on the school committee chaired by Dr. Luther V. Bell from McLean Asylum. He forged

First board of mayor and aldermen, and officers, 1872.

Advertisement for John P. Squire and Company's Somerville-Cambridge slaughtering plant.

a long-term relationship with the volunteer fire department, taking on the office of clerk as he worked closely with Nathan Tufts, the first chief engineer. During his term in the state senate, he was known as the genial friend of every man in the chamber, no matter what his political bent.

Along with Enoch Robinson, his neighbor on Spring Hill, Brastow and his friend G.T. Hill became the directors of the Somerville Horse Railroad in 1859. Connecting with the Middlesex Railroad at the eastern end of the town, the horses drew cars over Washington, Milk (Somerville Avenue) and Elm Streets. In 1863, the line was extended to Union Square, Somerville Avenue and East Cambridge. It was a natural extension of Brastow's commitment to provide homeowners and renters with better access to other parts of the city and Boston.

Defense of the town was another one of Brastow's preoccupations. As a founder of the Somerville Light Infantry in 1853, he built up a well-organized militia. By 1859, he was in command, urging able-bodied citizens to join, aware that a civil war was likely. On April 17, 1861, Captain Brastow called a town meeting in order to devise a plan to care for the families of the men who would be going into battle. A fund of over $5,000 was collected upon subscription. The Somerville soldiers marched out as Company B of the Fifth Massachusetts Regiment. During his three-month campaign, and later as paymaster, he was noted for his watchful oversight of the men under his charge. Many of these veterans would be among his staunchest supporters in the years to come.

Brastow's "hold on the people of Somerville was not gained by the display of any rare intellectual or moral qualities, but by his familiar social standing with the people and his self-sacrificing generosity." In 1872, on the night of his election as the first mayor, a local reporter went to interview the new city's premier politician at his home. Brastow was holding open house for his supporters. Many young boys, attracted by the celebration, hung about the yard. Some of the guests, quite a few of them ex-army buddies, decided that the boisterous teenagers were in the way. The reporter busily scribbled down the scene as Brastow rushed to the door, exclaiming: "Here! Don't drive away the boys! Why, men, these boys will soon be voters!"

Mayor Brastow's term was characterized by dealing with the problem of J.P. Squire's slaughterhouse and the pollution of the Miller's River. Mr. Squire had purchased land in 1855 on the East Cambridge side of the river for his business, which had expanded greatly by the 1870s. The slaughtering of thousands of hogs every week turned the stream, which was the fishing and bathing place for that part of Somerville, into a fetid mess. Adding to the nuisance was another slaughterhouse, North Packing Plant, and several sausage factories. Since the Miller's River was tidal, flats exposed at low water were covered with decomposing animal waste. The smells coming from the live hogs in the holding areas and the scalding water dumped into the river from the processing vats were compounded by noxious gasses that polluted the air.

The intolerable stench of the Miller's River basins drove the first city government to take aggressive measures—the river lowlands must be filled and an adequate sewer system built. All of this promised to be enormously expensive and increased the certainty of lowering yet another Somerville hill. At one of the first hearings before the

Massachusetts State Board of Health, Mayor Brastow was summoned to give testimony concerning his plan to alleviate the problem.

> *I am getting old and gray-bearded, and I don't* [alter] *my opinions easily, unless I have some basis to change them upon…My theory has always been that the basins should be filled and sewered, and I am not going to change it!*

Somerville joined with Cambridge in asking the legislature for power to compel Squire to do the work. Squire fought back and the measure was initially defeated. After two years of debate and negotiations, legislation was finally passed, whereby the landowners filled in the offending basins while a trunk sewer was constructed by Somerville and Cambridge, being completed in 1876.

George O. Brastow was the right man to change the role of Somerville from town outlook to city mentality. His ability to look forward to a bright future helped Somerville believe in itself. A confirmed optimist, Brastow believed that everyone could work together; it just took time, effort and a willingness to believe in the good found in others.

ENGINEERING HISTORY

Steeped in the Revolutionary War heritage derived from both his great-grandfathers, Charles D. Elliot (1837–1908) understood that history was more than a collection of dates. Born in Foxboro but living in Somerville since 1846, he attended the public schools and then studied civil engineering, associating with Daniel A. Sanborn, the mapmaker. As a topographical engineer in the Civil War, he was invaluable in building fortifications and in reconnaissance. Elliot returned home to oversee the Arlington Water Works until being appointed engineer to the new city of Somerville.

Elliot's interest in history served him well as he drew up the plans for the improvement of Central Hill in 1874. As a historian, he took unique pleasure in the fact that this hilltop, the scene of a Revolutionary redoubt, would remain forever open for the enjoyment of all the people. Extending his reach beyond city hall, he conducted surveys for the building of the Cape Cod Canal, plotted out the proposed Mystic Valley Parkway and became active in the real estate boom by managing and developing several estates. He was passionate about improving the streets, sewers and sidewalks in order to bring Somerville up to the standards of a modern city. Elliot also brought his sensible yet committed outlook to the Somerville Historical Society. Through his carefully written essays, he set a high standard for local writers who contribute to the *Historic Leaves*, its official publication. Finally, he was a firm believer that "the government and public service of a city reflect the character and intelligence of her people."

Charles D. Elliot was the city's chief engineer, president of the historical society and a successful real estate developer.

BRAVERY IN BRONZE AND STONE

Originally, the Central Hill Park area was owned by the Congregational Unitarian Society of Charlestown dating back to 1788. The land was called the "Church Lots" and was located on what was first named Middle Lane, then Church Street and, finally, Highland Avenue. Jacob Sleeper, a Boston merchant, purchased some of the parcel for investment purposes. When Somerville paid him $38,000 for it, the usual outcry arose, with some citizens complaining that the town needed to spend its money on better roads, while others were appalled that Prospect Hill was not chosen as the most logical place for the municipal buildings and a park. They reasoned that the land would have been cheaper and the view better. The selectmen were adamant:

> *This purchase definitely settled the question of a recognized center. This question no longer being in dispute, plans for the future development of the town may be made with especial reference to this fact.*

Central Hill Park became the first dedicated parkland in a town jealous of its territory.

As the twentieth century dawned and the ranks of veterans thinned, the city was determined to immortalize further the achievements of Somerville's Union Military. Central Hill Park was the perfect location. A call to artists was made and drawings were submitted for a suitable memorial. After evaluating twenty-six entries, the committee of politicians and ex-soldiers selected the work of Augustus Lukeman of Stockbridge. Amid much ceremony on a very rainy afternoon in 1908, the classic sculpture was dedicated. Over eight feet tall, the heroic bronze figures depict a Somerville volunteer starting out for the front with Victory in the form of a winged female figure giving him protection and encouragement. The February 1989 *Globe* suggested:

> *No place in the country is richer in historic incident than Somerville, and her citizens are fortunate in having so appropriate a ground on which to erect an enduring memorial. Somerville was the first municipality in the United States to raise a monument to the Civil War, and it seems poetic justice that this new memorial will have such historic environs.*

SOMERVILLE'S DOUGHBOYS

Wild as chaos, strong for ruin, clothed in hate unspeakable—
So they call me—and I care not—still I work my
waste afar,
Heeding not your weeping mothers and your widows—
I am War!
But your soft-boned men grow heroes when my flaming
eyes they see,
And I teach your little peoples how supremely great
they be.
—*"War" from* Songs of War and Peace, *Sam Walter Foss (1899)*

SAXTON CONANT FOSS

World War I was one of the most violent and destructive wars in history. The Great War, or "World War," as it was known, would eventually involve thirty-two countries and result in an estimated forty million casualties. The United States formally entered the war on April 6, 1918. In declaring war, President Woodrow Wilson stated, "It is a fearful thing to lead this great peaceful people into war, into the most terrible and disastrous of all wars, civilization itself seeming to be in the balance."

Over four million American men—native born, naturalized or aliens—were called to active duty. By the summer of 1918, the United States was sending ten thousand soldiers to France each day. Among those called to duty was Saxton Conant Foss, son of famed author and Somerville librarian Sam Walter Foss. Saxton Foss was born in 1889 and graduated from Somerville Latin School in 1906 and Harvard College in 1910. He enlisted with the U.S. Army as a private in June 1917, a member of the Ninth Infantry Regiment, Second Division. A newspaperman by trade, Saxton's letters home provide a glimpse into the life on the front lines. Saxton wrote:

Have been at the front again, but under different conditions. We had to dig our own trenches at night and stay in them all day. The first few days they were rather shallow, but in a short time we got them deep enough so they made fairly comfortable homes. We became owls, only venturing forth at dark and crawling back into our holes before daybreak. Will not deny that I have been in danger, as Fritz has been pretty active of late, and shells have come near enough to me to scare me half to death, but I am still unhurt. If I do not soon have a bath, however, will be completely camouflaged, and doubt if you would recognize your once immaculate son...

Do not regret you cannot send me as many bundles as formerly, because we are obliged to carry all our earthy possessions with us on our backs when we move. You need not worry about me as I am in good health, and if I am in no greater danger than I have been will come home without a scratch. Yesterday a French lady cooked me a supper of French fried potatoes, eggs, bread and cheese, and I listed to a band concert. [June 18]

Have lived in the trenches, holes in the ground, on the sides of rocks, in cellars deep under the ground, and am glad to be back in the honest and goodness barn filled with real hay. Went through the whole thing without a scratch, but will not deny that I had several narrow escapes. The only souvenirs I carried away with me were a pair of German shoes and a German pipe. Jim Baldwin came out of it safely. I met a fellow yesterday named Henry Armstrong, who comes from Union Square, and who joined our company a short time ago. Cannot but think of you and M—have been and are chiefly the cause of carrying me through without harm, and I think I shall surely come back safe and sound for your sakes. [July 12]

Sadly, Private Saxton Foss never returned to Somerville. He was fatally wounded on October 9, 1918, after volunteering to flank a German machine-gun nest as his battalion moved forward. He was posthumously awarded the Distinguished Service Cross. Foss Park on Broadway is named in his honor. Saxton Foss was buried at Aisne-Marne American Cemetery at Belleau Wood in France.

CESARE ADOLPHI MARCHI

The Aisne-Marne American Cemetery and Memorial, northwest of Château-Thierry, contains the graves of 2,289 American soldiers including those who fought in the Battle of Belleau Wood in the summer of 1918. The cemetery chapel is built over the site of the former frontline trenches.

Surprisingly, buried just a few rows from Private Saxton Foss is another Somerville doughboy, U.S. Army Private Cesare Aldophi Marchi. Unlike Saxton's Yankee roots, Cesare Marchi's family emigrated from Italy in 1910 and made their home on Derby Street in Ten Hills. Cesare served in the Italian army in the early years of the war and then returned to the United States to enlist in the army in 1918. Cesare was assigned to the Twelfth Company, Third Battalion, and later serviced with Company H of the Fifty-ninth Infantry Division.

It was the end of May 1918. Paris was in a panic and millions of Parisians were fleeing the City of Lights. It seemed that nothing could stop the German advances. The army set up a line of defense at the nearby town of Château-Thierry, near the Marne River. Lieutenant Lambert Wood, Ninth Infantry Division, stated their objective clearly, "We are blocking the road to Paris. So we don't die in vain."

Private Cesare Marchi was listed as missing in action on August 23, 1918. His family would later learn that Cesare had died on July 19, 1918. According to written records at the time, Cesare was the first Italian-American to die in World War I. The Cesare Marchi Playground on Meacham Avenue was dedicated in his honor on June 25, 1935. Over three thousand people paraded from city hall to the family's home on Derby Street and then to Meacham Avenue. The ceremony included a wreath-laying by Cesare's niece Marie Marchi Bonello and fellow soldier Raymond Massa, who was with Cesare at the time of his death. The Cesare Marchi plaque was rededicated at the Healy School in 2001.

Cesare Aldophi Marchi, 1918. *Courtesy of Marie Marchi Bonello.*

Ten dapper Marchi brothers pose at Ten Hills. *Courtesy of Marie Marchi Bonello.*

GEORGE DILBOY

Only one day before the death of Cesare Marchi, another Somerville soldier, Private First Class George Dilboy, also died at Belleau Wood. On July 18, 1918, Dilboy, of the 103rd Infantry, 26th Division, died after attacking an enemy machine-gun nest. In his citation for bravery, Private Dilboy was praised for his gallantry and service beyond the call of duty. After his platoon had gained its objective along a railroad embankment, Dilboy and his platoon leader went to inspect the ground beyond. Suddenly, they were fired upon by enemy machine guns. From a standing position on the railroad track, fully exposed to view, Private Dilboy opened fire. Failing to silence the guns, he rushed forward with fixed bayonet through a wheat field toward the gun emplacement, falling within twenty-five yards of the gunnery with his right leg nearly severed and with several bullet holes in his body. With amazing courage, he continued to fire at the enemy from the ground, killing two and dispersing the rest. In 1921, Private Dilboy was posthumously awarded the Congressional Medal of Honor, America's highest decoration for valor—he was the first Greek-American to receive such an honor. General John Pershing called Dilboy one of the ten greatest heroes of the war.

A statue of Congressional Medal of Honor recipient Private First Class George Dilboy. The statue stands in front of city hall on Highland Avenue.

George Dilboy's short life was one of constant sacrifice. Born in the Greek village of Alatsata in 1896, Dilboy came with his family to America in 1908 and settled in Somerville. A year later, he returned to Greece to volunteer to fight with the Greek army. Returning to Somerville, he then volunteered to fight in the Mexican Border War and was honorably discharged. Within months of his discharge, he rejoined the U.S. Army to fight on the battlefields of France.

After his death, Private Dilboy was featured on Victory Liberty Bond posters and newspaper advertisements throughout the country, bearing the slogan "I'll Get Them, Sergeant." At his father's request, George Dilboy was buried at his birthplace in Alatsata. It is reported that over seventeen thousand mourners took part in his funeral procession. In 1922, the *New York Times* reported that Turkish soldiers had broken open Dilboy's coffin and desecrated the soldier's remains and an American flag. President Warren Harding was outraged. Harding sent a warship to Turkey to recover Dilboy's body. On November 12, 1923, Private Dilboy was buried with full military honors at Arlington National Cemetery.

On August 26, 1930, the George Dilboy Monument on Central Hill Park was dedicated. The Dilboy Field and its stadium were named in his honor.

Chapter 5

Winter Hill

BECOMING RESOURCEFUL

Two Generations, Two Points of View

Charles A. Forster's (1798–1866) reputation as a philanthropist was legendary in Charlestown, his birthplace, and then in Somerville. The story was often told that he would give a dollar to any man who claimed that he was poor. Forster was also a skilled furniture maker by trade. He failed in business but eventually paid off all his creditors. At the time of the convent burning on Ploughed Hill, he was serving as one of the Charlestown representatives to the legislature.

When Forster moved his family to the estate on Sycamore Street—at the corner of Broadway, on Winter Hill—he became a powerful advocate of public education. His work on the school board was enlightened yet practical. Politically, he was an ardent abolitionist and temperance reformer. He also persuaded the town government to plant many of the trees on the newly constructed Winter Hill streets. The *Somerville Journal* commented, perhaps a little wryly, that he was so charitable that he came near to leaving his own family in poverty when he died. A grammar school was named in his honor amid much celebration.

Charles Forster, the son (1826–1901), became a brilliant entrepreneur. He inherited his father's magnetic personality, but not his philosophy. Charles worked to attract money rather than to disperse it. On a business trip to Brazil, having been hired by an import/export firm, Forster noticed that the natives chewed on toothpicks. Everyone chewed, including children and old men. The American duly noted the national pastime. Forster returned to Boston and found that his fiancée, Charlotte Bowman, was about to make a most fortunate purchase.

Charlotte, following up on the Brazilian toothpick story, was about to buy a patent from Benjamin Franklin Sturtevant. Already a successful inventor of a shoe-pegging machine, Sturtevant had also developed a toothpick-making device. Unfortunately, Sturtevant could not find a market for the millions of toothpicks that he could produce. No one wanted something that was not in demand. Mr. and Mrs. Forster stepped in and relieved him of his patent. Now the question came of how to make the toothpick a valuable commodity.

Forster targeted small local businesses, a prominent one being the Union Oyster House in Boston. He hired young men, especially Harvard students, to frequent the establishments and ask for boxed toothpicks when leaving. Of course, the storekeepers or restaurant owners could not provide them. Almost magically, Forster or his representative would drop by to sell the product to the eager businessmen. The same hires would then return and repeat their experience. This time the retailers were prepared. Success all around.

The young men would give back the toothpicks to Forster, who would then resell them to the businessmen. A fad became a trend, which became an industry. By the 1880s, chewing toothpicks in public was a fashion statement. Brazil and Greater Boston finally had something tangible in common.

After perfecting the toothpick-making process, Forster and family moved to Dixfield, Maine, which was situated in the midst of a prolific birch tree belt. Birch was the ideal raw material for the new industry. Employing over two hundred men and women in his factory, Forster made Dixfield into one of the wealthiest villages in New England. After his death, the business was continued by his son Maurice. No one in the family worried about being left penniless. The first Charles Forster would never have dreamt that a fortune could be built out of little slivers of wood.

THE WEDGE WITH THE GREAT VIEW

At the top of Winter Hill, there are two roads that define a wedge of land. On the left, Broadway continues over the hill into Ball Square, Powder House Circle and on to Tufts College. Main Street, on the right-hand side, soon crosses the city line into Medford, passes by the Royall House and terminates in Medford Square. This slice of real estate offers a spectacular view of Bunker Hill with the violet edges of Boston buildings shimmering in the distance. From the early days of Somerville, no one doubted that this spot would contain layers of stories.

Just before the Revolution, this location spurred the colonists to set up a quick formation of breastworks. It was a natural line of defense because it was a nexus to the interior. Paul Revere galloped over Winter Hill to Main Street when raising his alarm in April 1775. A day later, the British marched by on their way to Lexington. Anne Adams Tufts, living on Broadway, left the heights of Winter Hill to rescue soldiers wounded in the Battle of Bunker Hill in June. George Washington commented that

> upon my arrival [in Boston], *I immediately visited the several posts occupied by our entrenchments on Winter and Prospect Hills…The enemy's camp* [is] *in full view, at a distance of little more than a mile.*

Several decades later, Colonel John Sweetser was determined to build an imposing mansion on the site in 1805. He favored large, high-studded rooms with ornate marble mantels and fireplaces. He planted gardens that flowed from the rear of the house

The house occupied by Edward Everett (also known as the Odin-Hittinger House) on Winter Hill, now the site of the Paul Revere Apartments. Historic Leaves, *1903–1915.*

almost to the summit. In the spring, the orchard of pear and apple trees were covered with white blossoms. His signature piece was the wide front piazza that offered an unexcelled view of the surrounding countryside. The landmark mansion became known as the Odin house, named after one of the first owners. A local story hinted that at one point it might have been a tavern or inn.

When Edward Everett moved in during 1826, the elegant mansion had found its human counterpart. Everett was eloquent, passionate and expansive. Although he studied to be a clergyman, he had opted to become a politician and was representing Somerville in the U.S. Congress. He needed to live in the district and the most outstanding house on Winter Hill was ideal.

As the youngest member of Harvard's class of 1811, he was blessed with "brilliant natural endowments such as systematic and tireless industry, and a marvelous memory." He became an orator of surpassing eloquence. Everett's fame was so widespread that former president John Adams referred to him as "our most celebrated youth." Having courted and won Charlotte, a daughter of Medford's fabulously wealthy Peter Chardon Brooks, he had also selected the house because it was located on the road to his wife's girlhood home at Mystic Grove.

The Everetts loved to receive guests. Shortly after settling in, they began to have visits from Charles Francis Adams, the young Boston lawyer who was the son of the current president. On a prolonged trip to Washington, C.F. Adams had mingled in

Paul Revere's ride, Somerville Centennial Celebration, 1972. *Courtesy of the Somerville Public Library.*

the social circles befitting a son of President John Quincy Adams. Abby Brooks, the youngest daughter of Peter C. Brooks and sister of Charlotte Everett, was also part of the Washington scene. It had been love at first sight. Now Charles was in the process of courting Abby and stopping by the Everett mansion for tea and words of wisdom because Mr. Brooks enjoyed placing obstacles in the path of any potential suitor. The courtship lasted over two years, so the trips back and forth to Medford were as frequent and predictable as Charles's swings between hope and despair.

Even though Everett's job in the House of Representatives kept him away from home for months at a time, he did interact with his neighbors. In one brief note, he ordered delivery of hay from Captain John C. Magoun, a prosperous farmer and milk dealer, whose seventy-one acres were diagonally across Broadway. Other Winter Hill residents informed him of local events. After Everett had moved from the neighborhood, Magoun's house would become the safe haven for the nuns and pupils fleeing the burning convent (1834).

Everett sold the mansion in 1830 and went on to serve as a president of Harvard and governor of Massachusetts. Today, he is probably most remembered as the long-winded orator who preceded Abraham Lincoln at the dedication of the cemetery at Gettysburg during the Civil War. The next day, Everett, to his credit, sent Lincoln a note, congratulating him on his brevity and eloquence.

Somerville's smallest park, Paul Revere Park, commands the corner of Broadway and Main Street on Winter Hill. Photograph 2008.

John S. Edgerly was the next owner. Active in city government, he earned the nickname of "Winter Hill Eagle" because he lived at the summit of the highest hill in Somerville. Another notable occupant was Michael Hittinger, who bought the house in 1866. Hittinger, an organizer of the Fresh Pond Ice Company, was a tycoon who specialized in shipping ice to the West Indies. He removed the piazza, adding a porch and high, square tower. Ships in the harbor could be easily discerned from the new observation point. The house was the preeminent mansion on the hill, but its fate after the Hittingers took a turn for the worse.

At the beginning of the twentieth century, James M. York purchased the mansion at public auction, along with some of the back acres. A number of building lots had already displaced the rear orchard. York was not eager to live in the house but considered remodeling it an investment. Nothing came of that plan, which led to the landmark being abandoned and quickly falling into decay.

After years of neglect, the highest point on Winter Hill began to morph. The large lot filled with pine trees that fronted the mansion interested Frederick Rindge, the wealthy benefactor of Cambridge Rindge and Latin School. He bought it and then sold the tip of the wedge to the city. The city eventually widened the street at the junction of Broadway and Main Street. The remaining piece of land was turned into a parklet honoring Paul Revere. Arguably getting the most out of the least space, Somerville erected memorial tablets honoring the Revolutionary entrenchments, Revere and Anne Adams Tufts, the heroine of Bunker Hill. A single pine tree now commemorates the grove that once grew there.

James York found that he owned an 1805 dinosaur of a house and could not wait to get rid of it. John A. Walker of Medford and his brother saw the modern possibilities of the site. This was the ideal place for an ultramodern apartment building of forty units with the potential of adding twenty more. On March 16, 1912, the work of demolishing the old yellow mansion began. Up rose the Paul Revere Apartments, which—like the Princeton farther down Winter Hill—featured the latest in conveniences such as Murphy beds and ironing boards that folded into closets.

A VIEW FOR EVERYONE

The *Somerville Journal* of 1885 was congratulatory and hopeful. In process of construction—close to Charlestown, yet within the limits of East Somerville—the walls of a splendid great brick apartment hotel were fast piling up, the first ever built in the city. Located on Perkins Street and bounded by Mt. Vernon Street, it would be surrounded by a circular drive, which would also have access to Mt. Pleasant Street.

> *A more convenient locality could not have been chosen and, coming as it does at a time when rents are higher than ever before in Somerville, the hotel must be welcomed by the public and profitable to its owners.*

It was new, different and would prove unlike future apartment buildings.

Broadway, Winter Hill, looking east, 1905. Note the electric streetcars, horse-drawn carriage, automobile and bicycle in the distance. The Langmaid Terrace is on the left. *Photograph by Thomson and Thomson. Courtesy of Historic New England.*

The owners were women. Two Cambridge ladies, Mrs. S.D. Sargent and her sister-in-law, owned the land and building. The four-story structure would contain twelve suites with six rooms each. A special architectural feature would be the double circular staircases, with a separate staircase in the rear for the servants. Bay windows, a high central tower, hot and cold running water and private bathrooms would complete the amenities. This first edition of the Somerville apartment building would be generously spacious, elegant and similar to some of the new construction in the newer sections of Boston.

This brave new style would determine the landscape as it gained popularity. Gradually, some of the homes of descendants of Somerville's first families were moved or razed to accommodate the latest in modern living. Frederick C. Fitz, related to Anne Adams Tufts, Revolutionary War heroine, passed his early life at 335 Broadway. The Fitz home gave way to the Princeton Apartments in 1914.

Langmaid Terrace Apartments, Broadway, Winter Hill. Photograph 2008.

THE SPICE MOGULS

The unexcelled firm of Stickney and Poor, spice merchants, was founded in 1815, just as peace was declared between England and the United States. With the motto of "Purity and Quality Unexcelled," they became the largest manufacturers of pure spices in the world. In 1839, there were thirteen mustard producers in Boston. By the time Rufus and John took control, their plant, located on Spice Street, Charlestown, was the only survivor. It was a Somerville tradition to pair a homemade ham sandwich (ham from North Packing or Squire's) with the tongue-biting taste of S&P mustard.

Rufus Stickney's ample house on Broadway, at the corner of Sycamore Street, was the scene of many social events. The family moved in all the right circles. His son, Rufus H., who worked with him in the business, was considered one of Somerville's most eligible bachelors. When he married Carrie Conant of Pearl Street, the *Journal* noted that they invited guests who were among the "better class of citizens."

Stickney controlled an impressive amount of real estate. At the corner of Marshall Street, he built the Masonic apartments and Stickney building in the area of Gilman Square.

As a prominent member of the Massachusetts Horticultural Society, John R. Poor (1818–1903) brought samples of his home-cultivated fruit to the meetings. He was very proud of his fine apple orchard that covered much of his property on Broadway at the corner of Dartmouth Street. Very popular in Somerville, he was almost elected the first mayor. Not successful in that bid, he did not hesitate to dedicate himself to the task of bringing reliable gas and water systems into the town. He initiated the plan to widen Broadway and School Street. When people started discussing the need for a park on Central Hill, he was in the lead. After working to establish the Franklin Street Church, the first religious building on Winter Hill, he turned his attention to developing some of his property, which embraced Thurston and School Streets over to Medford Street.

Upon Poor's death, Irving Whitcomb, one of the partners of Raymond and Whitcomb Excursions, moved in to the elegant residence on Broadway. Whitcomb was on the cutting edge of a trend that catered to wealthy Bostonians who wanted to go south or west in the winter in hopes of avoiding the cold. The rest of the estate was quickly divided into house lots, with the prize apple orchard being one of the first casualties. Four or five of the trees did survive for many years, softening the appearance of the new construction.

THE PICKLE MAN

Near the crest of Winter Hill was the home of Edward Foote (1824–98), a partner in the world-famous firm of Bunker Hill Pickles. At one time a farmer in Long Island, New York, he bought his house on upper Broadway in order to enjoy the invigorating air. He did not seek city office, but he did serve a lengthy term on the water board. Unlike some of his neighbors, he did not buy up acreage where he lived. The land for which he was steward was the brick pickle factory situated on Walnut Street off Broadway.

Edward Foote, in partnership with George Skilton, manufactured Bunker Hill pickles at the top of Winter Hill.

By the 1890s, those who lived nearby were complaining of the obnoxious smell coming from the premises. Established in 1860 by the Skilton family, who had once lived in a house adjacent to the factory, the plant contained sixty vats involved in production. The wastewater and the disinfectants used to treat the equipment were discharged into sewers. Gases and smells of onion, vinegar and chloride of lime were drifting up from the manhole covers. It was not said, but implied, that the neighbors were also indignant that the owners lived in an area not impacted by industry.

At a public hearing, lawyers for the company asked if anyone had noticed foul odors coming from the clothing of the girls who worked in the factory. These young women rode public transit, mixing with other middle-class residents. When responding in the negative, protestors were urged to examine the stench emanating from the Kenneson pigpens not fifteen feet from the building. The board of health took the testimony under consideration, having already been busily involved in complaints concerning problematic industries such as the slaughterhouses.

THE DIAMOND-STUDDED DEVELOPER

Halfway up Broadway was the Horace Partridge House with its very large cupola offering views of the Boston skyline. A wealthy sporting goods merchant, Partridge loved to acquire land and mold it to his own use. In the early 1870s, he was never one to pass up a bargain, especially when he could buy up many of the small homes that dotted the brickyard section of what would become Broadway (Foss) Park. They had to be moved or demolished, since the area was below grade and needed to be filled in. In a very economical way, they provided an instant buildup for the property he was developing.

His favorite accessory was an enormous diamond pin attached to his starched shirt front. When some of his hired help were grading his land or building more French-roofed cottages, he would join in the work, his diamond sparkling in the sun. People joked that he used some of his packing cases in the construction. While developing Partridge Avenue, Jenny Lind and some of Vernon Street, he built a small brick lab for his new son-in-law, "Willie" Nickerson, who would invent the razor marketed by Gillette. Rather flashy himself, Nickerson, a Massachusetts Institute of Technology (MIT) grad, was one of the first men in Somerville to own a bicycle.

A BRUSH WITH DESTINY

Alfred Carl Fuller was born in 1885, on a farm in the Canadian town of Grand Pre, Nova Scotia. The eleventh of twelve children born to poor but hardworking parents, Fuller attended grammar school, but never went to high school. In 1903, at the age of eighteen, Fuller left Canada to join brothers and sisters in the States. In his autobiography, Fuller wrote:

> *Several brothers and sisters had already shown one way to escape from the ox-team culture of the Annapolis valley into the modern world of the States. They took the "down" train from Berwick to Yarmouth, the night boat to Boston, and the Boston elevated cars to Somerville.*

A Few of Our Leaders in Household and Toilet BRUSHES

No. 1

SOMERVILLE BRUSH CO.,
236 Washington Street
SOMERVILLE, ❧ MASS.

Established in 1906, the Somerville Brush Company was later renamed the Fuller Brush Company, which is still selling its products door-to-door today. *Courtesy of the Somerville Public Library.*

In Somerville, the Fuller family had a small amount of success. One brother, Robert, operated a small express company, one was on the police force, another was a trolley conductor and the last sold household brushes until he contracted tuberculosis and died. As an immigrant, Alfred Fuller's early years were difficult. He lost three jobs as a train conductor, a handyman and a wagon driver. In 1905, he took a job as a brush and mop salesperson. Fuller liked this work and managed to save $375, which he used to start his own business, the Somerville Brush and Mop Company.

Fuller set up a workshop in the basement of his sister's house and spent eighty dollars on equipment. On a bench between the furnace and the coal bin, Fuller constructed wire brushes. He made his brushes at night and sold them door-to-door during the day.

By 1910, the Fuller Brush Company employed twenty-five salespeople and six factory workers and had reached $30,000 in sales. Fuller Brush made a variety of products, including mops, brooms, hairbrushes, toothbrushes and combs. By 1919, the company had made $1 million in sales.

In 1921, the *Saturday Evening Post* magazine coined the term the "Fuller brush man," and it quickly became a part of the language. Fuller Brush become such an institution that two movies, *The Fuller Brush Man* (1948) and *The Fuller Brush Girl* (1950), placed lead actors Red Skelton and Lucille Ball in the role of Fuller salespeople. The Walt Disney film *The Three Little Pigs* even showed the big bad wolf approaching the pigs' house dressed as a Fuller brush man. Female salespeople, called "Fullerettes," were added in the 1940s to help market cosmetics. In 1960, Alfred Fuller published his autobiography, *A Foot in the Door: The Life Appraisal of the Original Fuller Brush Man, as told to Hartzell Spence*. In 1968, food giant Sara Lee bought the company. Alfred Fuller died in 1973. At the time of Fuller's death, the Fuller Brush Company's income was $130 million annually.

In addition to Alfred Fuller, Somerville flowed with the entrepreneurial spirit. Other famous companies got their start in Somerville.

THE MILK MAN

Harvey Perley Hood moved to Somerville in 1844 from Vermont and was hired to drive a bakery delivery wagon. Two years later, he bought a milk route and began home delivery of milk. Hood hired its first food scientist in 1894, and within a year it became the first dairy in New England to use pasteurization. Hood pioneered glass bottles in 1895, and later became the first American dairy to produce frozen yogurt. H.P. Hood is still a New England icon. While Hood has vacated its large building along Interstate 93 in Somerville, the building is still referred to as "the Hood plant" by traffic reporters and older residents. Hood and other local businessmen founded the beautiful Prospect Hill Congregational Church in 1887.

THE SODA GUY

Charles Elmer Hires was a pharmacist from Philadelphia who is said to have invented Hires Root Beer on May 16, 1866. But Hires has a Somerville connection. Hires's obituary says that the Reverend Dr. Russell Conwell, the founder of Temple University (originally the Conwell School of Theology), and one-time resident of Somerville, asked Hires to help him concoct a beverage that might be sold among hard-drinking Pennsylvania miners in the interest of the temperance movement. Hires, who was studying medicine at Jefferson Medical College at the time, was happy to help. Conwell, smitten with the results, convinced Hires to call it a "beer," instead of a "tea," feeling it would be an easier sell to the working class. Hires would become the largest manufacturer of the soft drink "root beer" in the world.

In Somerville, Colonel Russell Conwell practiced law, speculated in real estate, entered into politics and began the publication of the *Somerville Journal*. Mrs. Conwell was equally popular and busy in social and religious circles, conducting a women's department in the *Somerville Journal* and raising two children, Nima and Leon. Leon Conwell would become mayor of Somerville.

A Sweet Fellow

In 1917, Somerville resident Joseph Archibald Query invented a special formula of marshmallow crème with a lofty consistency. Making the product in his own Springfield Street kitchen, Query sold the product door-to-door and it became a local classic. Query sold his recipe to Allen Durkee and Fred L. Mower for $500. Durkee and Mower began selling the product, "Toot Sweet Marshmallow Fluff," and later just "Marshmallow Fluff." The product is now sold in eighteen nations around the world. Durkee-Mower's Fluffernutter has been proposed at least once as a candidate for the official sandwich of Massachusetts.

An Education at Your Doorstep

In 1903, brothers Myron and Edmund Fisher founded Fisher College, originally the Winter Hill Business College. They located their school in the former home of businessman Rufus B. Stickney on Broadway in Winter Hill. Originally trained in a normal school in Iowa, the brothers sought their fortunes in the East, believing the growing numbers of immigrants needed a way out of their unskilled labor. Like the Fuller brush man, brothers Myron and Edmund sold their courses door-to-door on the streets of Somerville. The college offered a completely individualized curriculum in which each student could study whatever he needed to land the job he was seeking. Today, Fisher College is located in Back Bay, Boston.

A calendar advertisement for the Fisher School, 374 Broadway, now Fisher College. The Fisher School was established in 1903 as the Winter Hill Business College. *Courtesy of the Somerville Public Library.*

Chapter 6

Spring Hill
BECOMING EQUAL

THE BICYCLE GIRL

The advent of the bicycle was a cultural breakthrough for middle-class Somerville, especially the women. In the 1800s, using a "wheel" was more than a recreation, it provided a quicker means of transporting students to school and workers to their offices or factories in different parts of the city or to Boston. Understandably, the bicycle offered day-trippers a chance to ride to the Middlesex Fells or to picnic spots along the Mystic Lake. But as more bicycles appeared in larger and larger numbers, their use crossed barriers of gender and age.

Mrs. J. Rush Green of Cambria Street was celebrated as the first woman in New England to ride a bicycle. When interviewed by several newspapers in 1896, she explained that her odyssey started in 1888. At that time, she admitted, very few women rode and most men were still timid in taming the bicycle. Her husband enjoyed the sport, however, thus making her determined to learn the skill. After days of practicing in her yard, she took to the street with her specially designed wheel, which was shorter than her husband's. Accompanied by her male escort, she calmly pedaled through the neighborhood. It took a great deal of mental courage for her to ignore the stares and comments of the curious—especially the boys—who gathered to watch her progress.

So popular was bicycling that clubs of wheelmen formed in Somerville and surrounding towns. Scores of adult men gathered several times a season to participate in organized rides through New England. The clubs even joined as a unit in patriotic parades throughout metro Boston. As time went on, women insisted on creating their own bicycle societies. The Woodbridge Cycle Club, meeting at the Woodbridge Hotel in Davis Square, was composed exclusively of the wheelwomen of Somerville, Cambridge, Allston and Arlington. The ladies extended the warm hand of friendship to several male groups, who returned the favor by presenting the women with a club pennant and several gifts. Women embraced riding because it offered them mobility and independence.

The bicycle provided the "new woman" with mobility and independence. Photograph, August 1893. *Courtesy of Maynard and Laverne Batchelder.*

Her Point of View

"Why does not Somerville have a woman's club?" wrote journalist Barbara Galpin in 1894. In less than one week, an organization, the Heptorean Club, was formed, and it would become one of the strongest women's organizations in Massachusetts. Only two years after Galpin's call to action, the club boasted 350 active members and a waiting list of 160. The *Journal* noted the club's ability to unify Somerville,

> *bringing its different scattered sections together into closer and more friendly relations, and, with the exception of the hospital, there is nothing which so unites the best elements of Somerville life as this institution.*

The organization's main fundraising efforts were directed toward helping Somerville girls who graduated high school to attend college.

Besides its social value, Galpin thought a strong woman's club would also benefit a growing class of Somerville working women. She wrote:

Mrs. Anna D. West, president of the Heptorean Club, brought together women from all parts of the city for educational improvement.

A business woman connected with a club will make not only friends, but business patronage. The wider circle of friends she has, the more successful financially, she is likely to be.

A club would also provide social and moral support.

> *The greater part of her time is spent in struggle with bad bills, exacting customers, close bargains, and financial anxiety. She gets into a groove of worry out of which she is rarely jostled; and here is where the club proves a blessing. It takes her into a different atmosphere. The lighter vein of life is touched and she is rested, cheered, and made stronger.*

Getting Stronger

> *"Women are eligible to serve on school committees, and to vote at school meetings for members of school committees."*
> —*Massachusetts School Suffrage Law, 1883*

It had been a long, hard fight in the legislature for school suffrage law, and Somerville's own Mrs. Martha Ann (Perry) Lowe (1829–1902) was at the forefront. Martha was born in New Hampshire, but she moved to Somerville in 1850 with her husband, Unitarian Reverend Charles Lowe. At the age of thirteen, Martha lost both her parents and lived the remaining time with brothers and sisters in such far-off places as the West Indies and Spain. She was a graduate of Mrs. Segwick's Academy, a progressive school that prided itself on turning out independent, creative and socially conscious young women. With the coming of the Civil War, Reverend Lowe went south to serve as a chaplain to the Union troops and to work with the Freedman's Aid Society. His health, which was always delicate, suffered after the war, and he died in 1874 at the age of forty-five.

Martha Lowe continued to work for Unitarian causes, women's rights, temperance and African American and Native American civil rights. When the legislature passed the school suffrage act, she founded the Woman's Educational Union, with Mrs. Maria Theresa Hollander. Martha was its first and only president. The organization worked to advance the cause of woman and assist her in securing positions as physician, preacher, lawyer and school officer, for which, by training, she had a natural ability and moral character. The members were expected to visit their district schools, become familiar with their management and thus be able to vote intelligently for the members of the school committee. The Municipal Club was an outgrowth of the Educational Union, and it was specifically engaged in securing the registration of women, in order that they may vote.

Mrs. Lowe frequently participated in public gatherings and belonged to many social clubs. She was a frequent contributor to newspapers and magazines, and she published several works of poetry, including *The Olive and the Pine* (1859) and *Love in Spain, and Other Poems* (1867), and a biography of her husband, *Memorial to Charles Lowe* (1874). Mr. and Mrs. Lowe had two daughters, who married and lived in Somerville. Martha survived her husband for many years and died peacefully in her Spring Hill home on May 7, 1902.

Nurse and baby, ca. 1894. *Courtesy of Maynard and Laverne Batchelder.*

SOMERVILLE'S FIRST WOMAN OF THE NEWS

Barbara Galpin (1855–1922) knew firsthand the experience of being an independent working woman, a single parent and a trailblazer. Soon after graduating from high school in Claremont, New Hampshire, she married Henry Wallace Galpin. Mr. Galpin, many years her senior, was a wealthy merchant who promised to offer Barbara a secure life in which she could pursue her literary interests. He kept his word for three years, but his untimely death left her with an estate that was riddled with problems and a young child, George. Barbara was still a teenager.

Mother and son moved to Somerville, where Mrs. Galpin was fortunate enough to find a job as a typesetter with the *Somerville Journal*. Necessity and personal drive compelled her to succeed. Within a few months, she was volunteering extra hours in order to proofread news manuscripts, thus launching the *Journal*'s reputation for typographical excellence. Barbara entered the management side of the paper when she was appointed head of circulation and started editing some stories. Over the years, she carved out her own niche by writing special features for the *Journal* and the *Boston Globe*.

In a society dominated by male opinion, she wrote about issues that interested women. Her "Woman's Page" in the weekly was the first section turned to by Somerville

Mrs. Barbara Galpin, seasoned *Somerville Journal* newspaperwoman.

homemakers in all parts of the city. Mrs. Galpin focused on series of articles, especially travel in America and Europe. Her most interesting vignettes were published in 1892 under the title *In Foreign Lands*, in which she gave a lively description of sites in Paris, London, Rome and Venice, to name a few. The Somerville Historical Society highlighted one of her essays in its first official volume of *Historic Leaves*. In her spare time, she wrote verses, songs and lectures for women's clubs, historical societies and libraries; joined the Suburban Press Association; and worked on the Woman's Congress at the world's fair in 1893. One of her pieces in the *Journal* led to the founding of the Heptorean Club, the preeminent women's club of Somerville. As a charter member of the New England Women's Press Club, she was seen as a role model for young women striving to enter the world of journalism.

Living on Spring Hill at 137 Summer Street, Barbara devoted herself to her only son, George Henry Galpin. Her extensive private library provided him with an appreciation for learning. He attended the city's public schools and then went on to graduate from Harvard in 1897. His academic training led him to teach at Kenyon Academy in Gambier, Ohio. But the pull of Somerville was strong, causing Galpin to accept the position of assistant commissioner of public buildings. He then shared the house on Summer Street with his mother until he moved to New Haven, Connecticut, to teach in the high school.

In 1903, Barbara completed twenty-five years of service to the *Somerville Journal*. Her work on the paper was celebrated in a city-sponsored reception and dinner at the Hotel Vendome, Boston. Mayor Edward Glines, city officials, noted women of the state, prominent educators and personal friends gathered to applaud her unique career. Mrs. Galpin had come close to doing the impossible, given her time in society. She earned a salary, supported her child, achieved well-deserved recognition in her profession and yet did not forget her early years when she was financially desperate. She was a leader in many philanthropic and civic movements, always encouraging women to overcome difficult home and work situations. When she retired in 1920 from a lifetime of writing, she sold her home on Summer Street and moved in with her son in Connecticut. Upon her death in 1922, she closed a remarkable chapter based on independence, courage and talent.

> *Take the joys that lie nearest you, revel in them, lengthen them to their uttermost. Don't be forever looking off into the future for what may never come to you, for in that case disappointment is sure to be your lot, and crisis-climbing a constant exercise, which, while it may stimulate one's mental and moral caliber, is not the sort of labor destined to make the heart more contented.*

A LIVING LEGACY

> *"You can be poor, colored, and still help everybody."*
> *—Annie Johnson (WGBH, 1987)*

Annie L. Johnson (1904–95) graduated high school and worked as a domestic and in factories, while she and her husband raised eight children. In the 1960s, she began to help organize domestic workers through the Women's Service Clubs of Boston. She later co-founded the Union of Domestic Workers, which helped young women coming from the

South find work, better working conditions, workers' compensation and other benefits. As project director of Women in Community Service during the 1960s and 1970s, she guided disadvantaged young people to programs that taught them to become nurses' aides, clerical and sales workers, chefs and many other trade and office positions.

Mrs. Johnson was very active in Somerville civic groups. She was chairman of the Board of Health, a trustee of the hospital, president of the Somerville-Cambridge Elder Services and was active in the Somerville Public Library and the Democratic Committee. She was co-founder of Project Soup, a free supper program, helping with everything from buying food to cooking it herself.

In 1987, Mrs. Johnson, at the age of eighty-three, was honored with the Living Legacy Award presented by the National Caucus and Center on Black Aged in Washington, D.C. Past winners of the award have included Reverend Martin Luther King Sr., Roy Wilkins, Jesse Owens, Rosa Parks and Dr. Kenneth B. Clark. Mrs. Johnson's daughter, Pearl Morrison, was the first African American female principal in Somerville at the West Somerville Neighborhood School.

FIRST FAMILY CONFIDANTE

Marguerite "Missy" Alice LeHand (1898–1944) was the private secretary to President Franklin Delano Roosevelt for over twenty years. Marguerite was born in New York, but she came to Somerville as a small child with her parents. She attended local schools and graduated from Somerville High School in 1917. After graduation, she attended secretarial school and worked at the Democratic Party's national headquarters. In 1920, she was hired by Franklin Roosevelt shortly after his failed attempt to become vice-president and remained his secretary until 1941. She lived with the Roosevelt family at Hyde Park and then accompanied them to Washington when Franklin became the thirty-second president. In 1921, FDR suffered an attack of polio, and "Missy," as she was nicknamed by the Roosevelt children, accompanied the president to Warm Springs, Georgia, for his recuperation.

As the president's secretary, Missy's duties were numerous. She worked seven days a week much of the time, and was on hand at all hours of the day to deal with FDR's requests. She would daily meet with the president to go over his personal mail and prepare replies for him to sign. She managed the family's budget and took on many of the household responsibilities. In *FDR and Harry: Unparalleled Lives* (1996), author Robert Underhill states that Missy's role was more than a secretary. She was his constant companion and moral support.

> *She accompanied him on numerous vacations and trips to Florida and Warm Springs…She monitored his physical therapy, supplying humor to relieve the daily problems and pressures, and sharing his sailing and fishing expeditions, card games, and other recreations.*

A young Marguerite LeHand at home on Orchard Street, summer 1916. *Courtesy of the Somerville Public Library.*

Marguerite "Missy" LeHand and President Franklin D. Roosevelt in the White House Oval Office, 1940. *Courtesy of the Somerville Public Library.*

In 1973, in his book, *An Untold Story: The Roosevelts of Hyde Park*, Elliott Roosevelt asserts that Missy LeHand had an even closer relationship with his father. Elliott wrote:

> *Everyone in the close knit inner circle of father's friends accepted it as a matter of course. I remember being only mildly stirred to see him with Missy on his lap as he sat in his wicker chair in the main stateroom holding her in his sun-browned arms...He made no attempt to conceal his feelings about Missy.*

But the evidence to an affair seems very unclear. If not a personal relationship, her devotion to Roosevelt was steadfast. In his work, *Franklin Delano Roosevelt: Champion of Freedom*, Conrad Black notes that from 1925 to 1928, Roosevelt spent 116 weeks away from home for therapy; Eleanor was with him for 4 of those weeks, Missy LeHand for 110. Missy was said to have been very attractive, tall and slender, with beautiful, blue-gray eyes. She was briefly engaged to William C. Bullett, the future U.S. ambassador to Russia and France.

Missy may have also played a part in introducing a future New England legislator to the world of politics. During his high school years, Tip O'Neill played poker with Missy

LeHand's brother at their Orchard Street home. Later, while O'Neill was a student at Boston College, Missy invited him to Washington. Missy took him to meet the president and they exchanged small talk. O'Neill is said to have been surprised to see Roosevelt in a wheelchair and kept the news like a state secret, even from his own family. He considered FDR his idol and O'Neill recalled, "I truly believed in the philosophy of government that he believed in. That was what my ideals were all about."

In 1940, Missy suffered a debilitating stroke at the age of forty-five, and returned home to live with sister. After her stroke, Franklin changed his will to leave Missy half of his $3 million estate. Missy died in Somerville without ever knowing she was the beneficiary. At her passing, FDR noted to the *Somerville Journal*:

> *Memories of more than a score of years of devoted service enhanced the sense of personal loss which Miss LeHand's passing brings. Faithful, painstaking with charm of manner inspired by tact and kindness of heart, she was utterly selfless in her devotion to duty. Hers was a quiet efficiency, which made her a real genius at getting things done. Her memory will ever be held in affectionate remembrance and appreciation, not only by all the members of our family, but by the wide circle of those whose duties brought them into contact with her.*

Missy's funeral was held at St. John's Church in North Cambridge, and Eleanor Roosevelt attended the services. Missy is buried at Mount Auburn Cemetery in Cambridge. In 1976, Somerville Mayor S. Lester Ralph commissioned a portrait of President Franklin D. Roosevelt and Marguerite LeHand to hang in the Somerville Public Library.

ENOCH'S ROUND HOUSE: THINKING OUTSIDE THE BOX

Five years after Somerville became a town, Enoch Robinson was living in an ordinary frame house on Central Street. He was interested in a lot adjacent to a large tract of open land on Atherton Street. The southern slope of Spring Hill enjoyed particularly fine light, and Robinson wanted to capitalize on it. When he bought the property in the 1850s, the neighbors wondered what this creative but eccentric hardware dealer would build. For over two years, they watched the construction of a round house, which became a Somerville attraction and curiosity in 1856.

Robinson's new home was not the first example of his ability to create the unusual. Coming from solid Yankee stock, he inherited the mechanical ability of his immediate ancestors. Some had worked in southern Massachusetts producing gun parts, jewelry and glass buttons. His own brothers, George and Ezra, were highly successful in their brass foundry in Boston. As a young man, Robinson had trained in the employ of a ship trimmer and manufacturer of steering apparatus. Then he joined the New England Glass Company of East Cambridge in the 1820s. He could not accept the status quo and had to explore new possibilities, especially when the subject involved the magic of glass.

Enoch Robinson's round house. Photograph 1894. *Courtesy of Maynard and Laverne Batchelder.*

The round house was the site for a benefit for the Ladies' Aid Association. *Courtesy of the Somerville Public Library.*

Robinson appreciated the process by which molten glass in an open mold was stamped with a hand-held plunger, thus producing furniture knobs and other articles. Yet he believed that there had to be a more economical and accurate method to accomplish the same goal. He collaborated with Henry Whitney, a fellow worker, and invented one of the first glass-pressing machines in America. Despite the criticism of other glass artisans, the Robinson/Whitney creation was tried out successfully. It featured a bench press with a fixed lever that drove a die down with great force and control. All this was accomplished in one operation. The plunging die could have designs such as "circles, rings, hearts, roses, leaves, fruit, animals or any other ornamental shape." The patent issued on November 4, 1826, was a huge technological advance that revolutionized the glass industry.

When difficulties arose at New England Glass, he briefly joined his brothers at their brass foundry and locksmith manufactory. Ezra and John were also inventors, procuring several patents over the course of their careers. Breaking from them, Enoch established his own locksmith shop at Dock Square. The three brothers kept their family ties close when they all moved to the same Somerville neighborhood near Spring Hill in 1847. Enoch was the only one who decided to build a conversation piece.

The house was a perfect circle, forty feet in diameter. A solid stone foundation supported three stories, the third being stepped back. Not one timber was used. Instead, planks were sawed to fit the circular configuration and nailed one above the other. Adoniram J. Taylor, a master carpenter of Somerville, was hired to do the painstaking work of piecing the strips and constructing the windows, which were four large pieces of glass set in a sash. The windows, sliding up in cases between the outer and inner walls, had to be precisely placed. The ones on the second floor could not be directly above those on the first, otherwise, the bottom windows would have nowhere to retreat. The problem of opening the second-floor windows was solved by constructing a series of battlements on the smaller third floor. The battlements were not only ornamental, but also served as a sleeve for the window casements.

The interior of the house was equally unusual. The front vestibule was an odd shape bordered by the round exterior, a circular library and the oval of the parlor. In the library, Robinson installed two wall niches for books. Always the creative scavenger, he had rescued the niches from the demolition of a building in Boston. The parlor was decorated with European wallpaper depicting scenes of castles, gardens and royal hunting parties. A very elaborate chandelier with many pressed-glass pendants illuminated the sitting room. Undoubtedly, the chandelier was created by Robinson's glass-pressing machine. The doorknobs in several rooms were his trademark molded clear glass with white medallions in the middle. Some centers depicted flowers or presidents of the United States. Adoniram Taylor, besides being able to solve the puzzle of constructing a round exterior, contributed to the ornamentation of the parlor by supplying the wooden carvings of flowers and cupids that decorated the space above the parlor doors.

Robinson was content to stay on Central Street for about a year after the house's completion. He graciously opened his new home for the first time to a charity event. It was a stroke of genius that benefited the Ladies' Aid Association on Spring Hill. The ladies of the parish were delighted to sponsor a three-day fair culminating in a social levee. The opportunity to buy useful and fancy articles at the "Novel Edifice" was irresistible. Somerville residents could be charitable while gawking at the central skylight, the peculiar sliding blinds and the unique kitchen with its white wood and slate floor. In a grand gesture, out-of-towners were accommodated by special cars and omnibuses that would come from Boston every hour from 8:00 a.m. to 8:00 p.m.

Once the Robinson family moved in, they stayed. After about five years, a semicircular barn was built behind the house. The barn was demolished in the 1880s, but that was the only major change in the many decades that the family occupied the residence. The heavy front door, with its dog's head handle, became bronzed over time. The metal decorations along the ledges of the windows, the network of brass and iron above the first story and the iron balcony extending over the small front porch aged gracefully. Upon his death, Robinson left the house to two of his children for the support of his wife and his other daughters. Four of his sons continued his business on Cornhill, Boston, until the turn of the twentieth century.

A Boston interior designer of the 1890s described Robinson's work as "nice cut glass and brass knobs set like diamonds." Today, his hardware is treasured for its elegant craftsmanship. It can be found in private collections, as well as on some of the doors of the United States Treasury building and Boston's Omni Parker House. Fine reproductions are also available. The round house itself still exists, but it has been through difficult times and for years remained vacant. Because of Robinson's careful design and Taylor's skill, it has survived neglect and the onslaught of decay. In 2007, the round house was purchased. The new owner has promised that it will be completely restored. This latest development would be welcome news to Robinson, who firmly believed that a round house was more economical to build than a box-shaped one. More important, however, was its ability to bathe the interior in the wonderful light of Spring Hill.

Chapter 7

Prospect Hill and Union Square
BECOMING INSPIRED

On this hill
The Union flag with its thirteen stripes
the emblem of the
United Colonies,
first bade defiance to an enemy
Jan. 1, 1776.
Here was the Citadel
The most formidable works in the
American lines
during the Siege of Boston
June 17, 1775, to March 17, 1776.

PATRIOTISM AND PRESERVATION

In July 1775, General George Washington assumed his role as commander in chief of the Continental army. Taking command, he found the British entrenched on Bunker Hill. The Americans were entrenched at Winter Hill and Prospect Hill, lacking reinforcements, supplies and leadership. Washington went immediately to work building up fortifications along the siege lines. He placed the four thousand men camped on Prospect Hill under the command of General Charles Lee and took up his headquarters in Cambridge. A letter written by the Reverend William Emerson, a chaplain in the army, a few days after Washington's arrival gives some indication of camp life on Prospect Hill.

Thousands are at work every day from four till eleven o'clock in the morning. It is surprising how much work has been done. The lines are extended almost from Cambridge to the Mystic River; so that very soon it will be morally impossible for the enemy to get between the works…Who would have thought, twelve months past, that all Cambridge

Somerville Gateway mural in Union Square. The mural, painted by Somerville artist Be Allen, celebrates the raising of the first American flag by General George Washington on Prospect Hill. Photograph 2008.

and Charlestown would be covered over with American camps, and cut up into forts…My quarters are at the foot of the famous Prospect Hill, where such preparations are made for the reception of the enemy.

On July 18, 1775, Major General Putnam issued an order that all the Continental troops under his immediate command assemble at Prospect Hill. Putnam read to the gathered troops the new Declaration of the Causes and Necessity of Taking up Arms issued by the Second Continental Congress.

Our cause is just. Our union is perfect…With hearts fortified with these animating reflections, we most solemnly, before God and the world, declare, that, exerting the utmost energy of those powers, which our beneficent Creator hath graciously bestowed upon us, the arms we have been compelled by our enemies to assume, we will, in defiance of every hazard, with unabating firmness and perseverance, employ for the preservation of our liberties; being with one mind resolved to die freemen rather than to live slaves.

The whole army shouted their loud amen by three cheers, immediately upon which a cannon was fired from the fort.

On January 1, 1776, troops once again gathered on the hill. On this day, the colonial forces, composed of members of various militias and volunteers, were officially named the Continental army. General Washington ordered that the "Grand Union Flag" be raised on a seventy-six-foot schooner mast placed on Prospect Hill. Washington noted days later that the British may have gotten the impresson that the flag was a symbol of surrender.

We gave great joy to [the British] *without knowing or intending it, for on that day which gave being to our new army, but before the proclamation came to hand, we hoisted the Union flag in compliment to the United Colonies. But behold! it was received at Boston as a token of the deep impression the speech had made upon us, and as a signal of submission. By this time, I presume, they begin to think it strange that we have not made a formal surrender of our lines.*

But the American forces did not surrender. The Grand Union Flag flying on Prospect Hill continued to be a great morale booster for troops during the ongoing siege of Boston. The siege of Boston officialy ended on March 17, 1776. Prospect Hill continued to be used throughout the war. Near the end of the war, it was used as a prisoner of war camp for British troops, and in November 1777, over twenty-three hundred British troops captured at Saratoga were kept there for a full year.

ALMOST TOO GOOD

In the early days cows grazed on the pink clover growing on the summit, with a particular Gilson cow becoming distracted and falling off a ledge outcropping into the street below. The uninjured bovine enjoyed a minor star status. An old windmill managed by "Jimmie Cook" supplied meal to the locals while the mysterious G.W. Beck ran a Catholic boarding school for orphan boys. There was a rumor that he might have been the heir to the Swedish throne. During the Civil War some of the soldiers encamped on the hill searched for the site of the Revolutionary flagstaff so that they could plant their own flag in its place. The Gilson family supplied the Union recruits with corn, tomatoes and buckets of hot water. It was a place for unusual characters.

The more recent newcomers, such as Union Square merchant Richard H. Sturtevant, built houses that joined multitudes of other beautiful residences. Both fire chief James Hopkins (Summit Avenue) and police chief Melville Parkhurst (Columbus Avenue) enjoyed its tranquility. An 1882 *Journal* article gushed that Grand View Avenue was "thoroughly toney," while every new house on Aldersy Street exhibited details that were "architecturally and florally" significant. The view from the summit was, of course, spectacular.

Living in a yellow house with high steps leading down to Walnut Avenue, Mrs. Nancy Munroe and Robert, her affluent grain dealer husband, were regarded as one of Somerville's power couples, immersing themselves in church work and civic activities. Nancy could not resist describing her perfect world in a flattering essay, "Our Model Neighborhood":

> *Upon a pleasant hillside, there is our model neighborhood* [where] *the children are never any trouble. Here they play from dawn to dusk as they go from house to house and no fault is found.* [Adults] *treat their neighbors' children as they would have their own treated, and should the children fall out, the parents are not obliged to follow their example.* [1856]

The problem with Prospect Hill was that everyone loved it.

GETTING A PIECE OF THE HILL

Although the Miller's River nuisance in the 1870s did not impact the Prospect Hill area directly, curing the problem did. Digging into the hillside and carting away the soil in order to cover the offending lowlands greatly altered the contour of the land. As the partially removed summit became less desirable for afternoon picnics, the historically minded woke up to the reality that their heritage was disappearing. Talk surfaced of securing the remaining land for a public park, but for years no one did anything.

The number of new homes created another problem. Some, such as Mrs. Martha Sanborn, understood that the ongoing development of the hill would eventually

MUNROE STREET, EASTERLY END.

MUNROE STREET, WESTERLY END.

The paving of Munroe Street with the Prospect Hill mound without its tower.
Somerville Annual Report, 1902.

compromise its desirability. She had inherited a beautiful tract lying between Warren and Walnut Streets that attracted eager developers who made her enticing financial offers. She refused to part with it during her lifetime, but her children, facing different priorities in the 1880s, sold it off.

Believing that there was strength in numbers, a group of concerned citizens met at the *Journal* office in April 1896 for the purpose of establishing and maintaining a park. Calling themselves the Prospect Hill Park Association, they pledged "to agitate for the preservation of one of the most historical spots in the country." Three adjoining parcels of land, about two and a half acres, on the south side of Munroe Street were available. H.M. Thompson, an heir to one of the pieces, wrote to the *Journal* explaining his reasoning:

> *This communication is intended to call the attention of the city fathers to the fact that, since I have decided to make an organized attempt to sell, now is the proper time to consider the subject of buying.*

Realizing that time was of the essence, Charles W. Colman, as president of the association, and others gathered over five hundred signatures on a petition addressed to the city committee on public grounds. Mayor Albion Perry, in his inaugural address of 1897, urged the public to fund the purchase of the land that was

> *in a rough and unsightly condition, and the approach to it from Walnut Street furnishes a marked example of the thoughtless and haphazard methods pursued by some of our citizens in the development of private lands.*

In 1898, the *Journal* became strident when declaring that

> *the recent sale of two lots of land directly opposite the proposed Prospect Hill Park for the purpose of erecting houses shows that there is a real danger of losing the site unless it is taken at once. In another year it would probably be too late to preserve this historic spot.*

The preservation of the hill was due in great part to the Randall and Gilson families who had never been in favor of cutting off the summit. Rejecting the offers of John P. Squire, the pork king, the two families sold their property to the city instead.

Through the efforts of the Improvement Society and Heptorean Women's Club, the Prospect Hill Park and Tower were built in 1903. Constructed according to the plans of city engineer Ernest Bailey, the tower stands at the original height of the hill.

A Visit from Walt Whitman

John Townsend Trowbridge (1827–1916) is most famous for knowing the famous. As a founding contributor of the *Atlantic Monthly* and a well-known writer of his day,

John Townsend Trowbridge raised social issues in his Civil War novels. *Early photograph from Trowbridge's autobiography,* My Own Story, *1903.*

Trowbridge made the acquaintance of many of America's greatest authors, including Ralph Waldo Emerson, Henry Wadsworth Longfellow, Oliver Wendell Holmes and Harriet Beecher Stowe—many of whom he entertained at his home in Prospect Hill.

John Trowbridge came to Somerville in 1858 to live with the Newton family in a small house at 12 Munroe Street. The household included Trowbridge, the Newtons, their three small children, a servant and fellow boarder, author Lewis Baxtor Monroe. Trowbridge wrote to his sister of his new home.

> All the divinities of my life seemed to conspire to put me here,—in one of the finest of our suburban towns, on the brow of a hill that commands a panoramic view surpassing anything you ever saw. The windows of the house overlook Boston…from the top of the hill, we can see a horizon that embraces sea, mountains, cities, villages, landscapes— wonderful to behold. We have the best country air here…I think I shall be as happy here as an old bachelor can be.

Trowbridge would not remain single for long, marrying Cornelia Warren in 1860. A son, Windsor Warren, was added to the household in 1864. The house was small and bustling, and perhaps not conducive for the work of writing. Trowbridge would find his inspiration, just steps away, on Prospect Hill. Trowbridge later wrote (1903):

> The old earthworks were my daily resort, and there on the loftiest embankment was for years a footpath which my solitary steps had worn and kept open, as in all weathers, under sun, or moon and stars, I paced that quarterdeck of the great ship sailing the universal deep. There I fashioned my poems or studied my plots (that of Cudjo among them), waling to and from, to and from, in the deepening gloom of evening, amidst a galaxy of near and innumerable distant lights, or by day, with many cities and villages outspread before and around me.

Trowbridge would write many popular novels: *Neighbor Jackwood* (1857) and *Cudjo's Cave* (1854), antislavery novels; *The Old Battle-Ground* (1859); *Coupon Bonds, and Other Stories* (1873); and *The Desolate South* (1866), a nonfiction account of Trowbridge's tour of Civil War battlefields.

One of the most well known of Trowbridge's houseguests was Walt Whitman. In 1860, Trowbridge was introduced to the author, who was in Boston to proof sheets of a new edition of *Leaves of Grass*. Trowbridge invited Whitman to share a perfect May afternoon.

> The next Sunday morning, he came out to see me on Prospect Hill, in Somerville, where I was then living. The weather was perfect,—it was early May; the few friends I introduced to him were congenial spirits; he was happy and animated, and we spent the day together in such hearty and familiar conversation that when I parted with him in the evening, on East Cambridge bridge, having walked with him thus far on his way back to Boston, I felt that a large, new friendship had shed a glow on my life.

The Prospect Hill tower captured on an idyllic day. *Original pastel by Somerville artist Charles McCarthy. Courtesy of Charles McCarthy.*

Walt Whitman. *Photograph from* My Own Story *by John Townsend Trowbridge, 1903.*

Of much of that day's talk I have a vivid recollection,—even of its trivialities. He was not a loud laugher, and rarely made a joke, but he greatly enjoyed the pleasantries of others. He liked especially any allusion, serious or jocular, to his poems. When, at dinner, preparing my dish of salad, I remarked that I was employed as his critics would be when his new edition was out, he queried, "Devouring Leaves of Grass?" "No," I said, "cutting up Leaves of Grass!"—which amused him more, I fancy, than the cutting up did that came later. As the afternoon waned, and he spoke of leaving us, the vivacious hostess placed a book before the face of the clock. I said "Put Leaves of Grass there. Nobody can see through that." "Not even the author?" he said, with a whimsical lifting of the brows.

At 15 Munroe Street, just across the street from Trowbridge, was the home of Henry Gilson, an agent for the Hartford Fire Insurance Company. Gilson often entertained local authors and writers. At the Gilson home, the first money for the Freedmen's Bureau (which supported the newly freed slaves) was raised at an evening of readings and music. John Townsend Trowbridge read from his own works, perhaps from his new antislavery novel, *Cudjo's Cave*.

For many of the residents of the hill, the Civil War was an inevitable conflict between good and evil whose time had come. William Schouler writes in his book, *A History of Massachusetts in the Civil War*:

The ladies of Somerville were forward in every good word and work for the soldiers, beginning at the commencement of the war and continuing until the end. They held meetings every week each religious society had its Soldier-Aid Society. They made under-clothes, scraped lint, sewed bandages, knit socks, roasted turkeys, baked pies, made jellies, and were unceasing in their patriotic and Christian work for the sick and wounded, and for the "boys of the cause." Even the unfortunate inmates of the McLean Insane Asylum, under the direction of Mrs. Tyler, furnished articles sufficient to fill four large boxes, which were forwarded to the front.

HISTORIC TALES

Elbridge Streeter Brooks (1846–1902) was born in Lowell in 1846, the son of Elbridge Gerry and Martha Fowle Munroe. His mother's family, the Munroes, owned the gristmills near the site of General Putnam's earthworks. Eldridge's great-grandfather, William Brooks, was a soldier encamped on Prospect Hill and fought at the Battle of Bunker Hill. Elbridge's connection to Somerville's patriotic past greatly influenced his writings. Elbridge made his home at 44 Walnut Street.

Brooks was the author of the series Historic Boys and Historic Girls, which appeared in *St. Nicholas Magazine* in 1885 and 1886. His books often mingled historical fact with playful imagination. Titles included *In No Man's Land*, *The American Indian*, *Wood Cove Island* and *Under Allied Flags*. About writing, Brooks believed *in leading children gradually, and that you cannot begin too early with healthful and instructive reading, especially that of a patriotic nature. One thing I never do, and that is "write down" to children; they know more than their elders give them credit for, and the proper way is to write to lift them up.*

Brooks was a member of the Authors' Club of New York, which included many of the leading writers of the day. He was a member of several historical societies and was vice-president of the Somerville Historical Society.

LIBRARIAN POET

Let me live in my house by the side of the road,
Where the race of men go by—
They are good, they are bad, they are weak, they are strong,
Wise, foolish—so am I.
Then why should I sit in the scorner's seat,
Or hurl the cynic's ban?
Let me live in my house by the side of the road
And be a friend to man.
—*"House by the Side of the Road,"* Dreams in Homespun *(1899)*

Sam Walter Foss (1858–1911), librarian and poet, was born in rural Candia, New Hampshire. He graduated from Brown University in 1882, and beginning in 1898, became the librarian at the Somerville Public Library. Always a booster for the average man and the importance of reading, Foss added to the library a children's room, a school department and a reference room. In 1887, he married Carrie Conant, a minister's daughter. They had two children, Mary Lillian "Molly" Foss and Saxton Conant Foss, who died on the battlefields of France.

Foss was an editor and regular contributor to local and national newspapers, including the *Lynn Saturday Union*, the *Yankee Blade*, the *Boston Globe* and the *New York Tribune*. He contributed poems and stories to the *Youth's Companion* and *Puck*, national magazines of the day. He wrote five books of verse: *Back Country Poems* (1893), *Whiffs from Wild Meadows* (1895), *Songs of War and Peace* (1898), *The Song of the Library Staff* (1906) and *Songs of the Average Man* (1907). He wrote his last newspaper column while in the hospital awaiting an operation that failed to save his life. The piece was entitled "Optimism."

Foss did not live in a rose-covered cottage, but on busy Highland Avenue in the center of town. Foss once said that when "he wanted country he had to ride the cars and pay his fare like everybody else." Foss's poems continued to be popular with the nation that rejoined in his celebration of the average man and his healthy cynicism of those in power.

In 1950, former first lady Eleanor Roosevelt used Foss's verse to voice her frustrations with Southern conservatives obstructing civil rights programs. In a letter to President

Librarian Sam Walter Foss and an assistant examine art books at the old library on Central Hill. *Courtesy of the Somerville Public Library.*

Harry Truman written on March 21, 1950, Mrs. Roosevelt suggested that the president read to some of the senators "A Calf-Path," a poem that mocks the willingness of people to blindly follow established traditions.

"A Calf-Path" (1895)

A moral lesson this might teach,
Were I ordained and called to preach;
For men are prone to go it blind,
Along the calf-paths of the mind;
And work away from sun to sun,
To do what other men have done.
They follow in the beaten track,
And out and in, and forth and back,
And still their devious course pursue,
To keep the path that others do.
They keep the path a sacred groove,

Along which all their lives they move.
But how the wise old wood gods laugh,
Who saw the first primeval calf!
Ah! many things this tale might teach—
But I am not ordained to preach.

MONUMENTS AND MEMORIES

Very early in the annals of Somerville's history was the establishment of the Milk Row Cemetery on Somerville Avenue. It was 1804, and Samuel Tufts generously donated a small piece of land that would take care of immediate need. The plots were individually owned, but, as the years passed, the general public was allowed to make use of the consecrated ground. Everyone realized that the overall space would soon become filled, leading to the necessary purchase of additional land.

Original sampler illustrating Sam Walter Foss's popular poem, "The House by the Side of the Road." *Private collection.*

"Their warfare is over, they sleep well." Civil War Soldiers Monument, Milk Row Cemetery, Somerville Avenue. The names of sixty-eight men who were killed in battle or died from wounds or sickness are inscribed on the four faces of the marble shaft.

By 1846, the town had followed up on the obvious by securing some acreage on Broadway for public burials. The 1858 Annual Report gently prodded the town by suggesting that this new area "must be dedicated for use unless our citizens shall judge it to be expedient to make some other provision." The selectmen were willing to repair the fence around the old cemetery, but they were reluctant to activate the Broadway site. There were more important things to do with the land. During the Civil War, the need became pressing. Enoch Robinson donated his own burial lot to use as a resting place for Somerville's fallen heroes.

The Somerville Light Infantry, aided by private contributions, erected a noble monument dedicated to the memory of those struck down in the three-month campaign of 1861.

The military memorial of 1863 served well, but space was still wanting. In 1865, the town report remarked that

> there is a vacant lot, but little used, belonging to the McLean Asylum. It is of suitable size, and it should be dedicated as the last resting place for the remains of the fallen heroes of Somerville, and it is hoped the Trustees of that institution will relinquish their claim in favor of the noble souls who have sacrificed their lives in the War.

Union Square, ca. 1915. Union Square was named for its role as a recruiting center during the Civil War. *Photograph by Thomson and Thomson. Courtesy of Historic New England.*

The report continued by scolding Somerville officials.

The town is still without a suitable place for burial. The Cemetery Board recommends the purchase of one. There is a desirable piece in Medford, near our line that we are told can be had at a low rate.

Despite the enticing prospect of getting a bargain, the Medford property was not obtained.

Somerville's cemetery did not expand beyond the original 1804 site. The problem also did not go away, especially as the population skyrocketed. A small area on Clarendon Hill, the Somerville Veterans' Cemetery, was later dedicated as a burial ground. Obituaries of the illustrious and the unknown shared a common denominator: burial was off-site. Many times, families returned the remains of loved ones to their birthplaces, where ancestors were interred. Sometimes, the lots belonging to relatives in surrounding towns were used. Frequently, Somerville residents purchased final resting places in fashionable cemeteries such as Forest Hills, where Fort Worth stockyard tycoon, Louville V. Niles, of Walnut Street is interred. Cambridge's Mount Auburn Cemetery received many Somerville notables such as Mayor George O. Brastow, McLean's Luther V. Bell, Columbus and Mary Tyler and several Tufts pioneers such as Hosea Ballou, Charles Tufts and President Capen.

CLEARLY ARTISTIC

A casual conversation in the early 1850s on a Cambridge wharf affected the lives of hundreds of Somerville residents. Amory Houghton (1813–82) happened to meet a British glassworker, "Gaffer" Teasdale, who intrigued the young contractor with his stories about the wonderful potential found in glassmaking. Houghton, already a seasoned carpenter and builder, had recently expanded his business interests to include real estate, plus trading in coal and wood.

Houghton was starting to diversify by becoming a part owner in a small glass company called Cate and Phillips, renamed Bay State Glass. He had regarded this investment as a prudent step, but not as a life-changing career move. Teasdale's inspired conversation encouraged Houghton to persuade his brother, Francis, and friend, John Gregory, to join forces in founding the Union Glass Works on Webster Avenue near Union Square.

Incorporated on January 21, 1854, the new company employed over one hundred men and boys. It was smaller than the New England Glass Works of East Cambridge, yet produced similar products. Situated next to the Fitchburg railroad, the company started with $60,000 in capital. During the first year, the skilled workers—many of them immigrants from the British Isles—created over $120,000 in glass items, most of which were wholesaled. The future looked very promising during 1856 as Houghton would walk from his Prospect Street home to the bustling factory.

Suddenly, in 1857, Somerville was thrown into the nationwide depression that followed an unexpected downturn in the economy. The financial panic that resulted caused businesses to fail, banks to close and unemployment to become rampant. As confidence eroded, a young company such as Union Glass Works could not withstand the economic blow. Business evaporated, leading to a reorganization of the company in an attempt to rescue it.

Amory Houghton was joined by his son, Amory Jr., who had set up a small laboratory on the property to begin his own experiments in glassmaking. Under new management, the company struggled along as the elder Houghton began establishing ties with the Brooklyn Flint and Glass Company. Around 1864, the Houghtons sold Union Glass in order to relocate to New York, where materials and labor were cheaper. Their last and final endeavor resulted in the founding of Corning Glass Works, which succeeded brilliantly.

Meanwhile, the glass factory was finally coming of age. John Haines, a superb craftsman, brought the art of silvering glass to the now solvent company. Other artisans devised a method of decorating, with gold worked into the glass rather than simply painted on the surface. A cutting department was added that employed more workmen to produce cut glass, which was sold in fine Boston stores. Pressed glass and blanks for use in other glass factories rounded out the lines. From 1870 to 1885, Union Glass (now) Company prospered, even when impacted by the emerging unions that championed the rights of the workers.

By September 1882, approximately sixty boys between the ages of fourteen and seventeen worked in the Somerville plant. Split into two teams or "gangs," they put in ten hours a day, with the more skilled receiving more pay per hour. The promotion of some workers caused discontent in the ranks. Going on strike for several days, the "youth walkout" crippled the flow of production. Management rethought the pay scale.

More important was the glass strike impacting New England in 1885. Throughout October and November of that year, fourteen out of fifteen of the Somerville chimney blowers refused to work, saying that their wages had been cut by 15 percent when the company asked them to sacrifice because times were difficult. They had endured debilitating conditions, they claimed, while making only seven to eleven dollars per week. As the strike lengthened, management offered to reinstate the men, but with the added caveat that the workers' union not be involved in any hiring or firing. After many negotiations, the union and the owners hammered out acceptable terms. Most of the workers had been employed at the glass company for many years, long before joining any organized union. It was a difficult learning process for the more than two hundred men, most of them living in Somerville on streets such as Holts Avenue, a private lane off Oak Street.

When Thomas Dana, a wealthy wholesale grocer from Cambridge, became president in 1891, the company was ready to move in a new direction. As the only surviving glass factory in metro Boston, the plant increased production of its fine flint glass pieces and glass doorknobs. In 1893, upon Dana's death, Julian DeCordova, his son-in-law, assumed management of the company. In a bold move, he improved the facility and

Italian immigrants became important to the Union Glass workforce. Others, such as newly married Nicola and Margherita (Capone) Dente, August 1915, enthusiastically called Somerville their new home. *Courtesy of Ed Dente.*

concentrated on the creation of lustrous art glass in the trendy art nouveau style. Under the direction of William S. Blake, a fine glass artist, the Somerville factory produced beautifully shaped and brilliantly colored pieces with the engraved trademark of "Kew Blas." Other artisans such as Philip Buonomo from Itri, Italy, were glass blowers and creators of specialty paperweights with lamp-worked words. These one-of-a-kind pieces were personalized to commemorate weddings, births and even deaths.

Union Glass Company at one point was the single largest employer in the city. Declared almost defunct several times during its more than seventy years, it survived a national panic, union unrest, strikes and changes in public taste. A 1905 *Globe* article offered the workers a well-deserved tribute:

> *Their skill has not been acquired quickly. There are men...now past middle life who went to work there as boys. Day after day and year after year they have been seriously practicing the difficult art, and none in their calling can excel them in skill.*

Chapter 8

Clarendon Hills and Wild Cat
BECOMING ENTHUSIASTIC

IT WAS THE '60S

During the Civil War, a large area on one side of Clarendon Hill was turned into Camp Cameron, a pre-deployment training base for raw recruits. The site had a split personality. Barracks and drill ground rested on a wide plateau in Cambridge, while the commissary, quartermaster's department and stables were situated on a sloping meadow belonging to Somerville. This broad field was cut by a small stream that then fed into Alewife Brook. Surrounding everything were the civilian neighbors.

Abby Paulina Simpson lived on the Somerville farm adjacent to the camp. As a young girl, she had seen the soldiers performing drills, maneuvering cannons and engaging in horseplay during their time off. Rather amazed at their boldness, Abby witnessed the Union boys making raids on her father's extensive vegetable gardens and fruit orchards. In September 1861, the thieves would have been soldiers from the First Massachusetts Light Battery, which was training for five weeks before leaving for the seat of war. Abby's father, a market gardener, was incensed that the source of his livelihood was disappearing before his very eyes. While appreciating the young men's patriotism, he welcomed the sunrise departure of the 152 soldiers as they marched off in their bright red, state-issued uniforms on October 3. In conversation with "Charlie" Tufts, a family friend and the benefactor of Tufts College, Farmer Simpson confessed that he had been able to retrieve some of his purloined squashes from the campgrounds. He could not rest easy for long, however, because other regiments, such as the exuberant Twenty-eighth Massachusetts Regiment, composed almost entirely of Irish volunteers, would train at Camp Cameron and further test his patience.

For the rest of her long life, Abby lived on her father's farm, finally dividing her portion by creating Paulina Street, named for her mother. In 1935, when she was almost ninety, she remembered many tidbits of history in an interview with the *Somerville Journal*. Two of her most interesting stories involved going to the dedication of Ballou Hall on July 23, 1853, and Charles Tufts's later visit to the Simpson farmhouse when he expressed his hope that any new college buildings would be constructed on the Somerville side of the line rather than in Medford.

CIVIL WAR ECHOES AND LEROY COUSINS

In 1896, one of the largest sales of real estate was announced, whereby Hicks and Townsend, developers, bought from E.K. Hall seventy-two house lots, including about 188,000 square feet, on the site of old Camp Cameron. The Cambridge section received street names such as Seven Pines, Malvern, Yorktown and Fair Oaks, commemorating important battles. Camp Street branched off Cameron, an interesting tree-lined street shared with Somerville. As the years passed, families of diverse backgrounds and races established their homes on or near the site that once resounded with the voices of Union soldiers.

On the next street of Elmwood, African American entrepreneur "Pop" Cousins was running a small variety store that also functioned as an informal community center in the 1890s. By the turn of the new century, William and Carrie Cousins were raising

Leroy Cousins, African American football star. LeRoy is in the top row, fourth from the left. *The Radiator (Yearbook), Somerville Latin and English Schools, 1907.*

their two sons, Leroy and Louis, at 47 Elmwood. Working as a night watchman for the Boston Elevated Railway Company, William wanted his sons to follow their own paths to success. Leroy discovered that his athletic abilities would serve him well. As one of the brightest stars of Somerville High School from 1907 to 1909, Cousins distinguished himself on both the baseball and football teams. The *Boston Globe*, in December 1908, applauded Leroy "Pep" Cousins's sportsmanship and dedication as he and other teammates received their athletic sweaters and the letter "S." In the next year, an article evaluating the quality of high school sports commented that the Rindge team from Cambridge would have a hard time checking Cousins, who was playing fullback.

When Leroy was a young man in 1915, Boston planned a great celebration of the fiftieth anniversary of the passing of the Thirteenth Amendment, the watershed legislation abolishing slavery. The Massachusetts Branch of the Equal Rights League and the Wendell Phillips Memorial Association organized a major public event, including speeches at Faneuil Hall and the placing of wreaths on the statues of Wendell Phillips and Charles Sumner, famed abolitionists. Leroy Cousins was appointed one of the parade marshals who supported the speeches urging the end to segregation, disenfranchisement and the establishment of fair play.

It Was a Blast in West Somerville!

One of the last neighborhoods to be developed, Clarendon Hill was a combination of cultivated acres, homes, a transportation terminal and the site of a stone quarry that became a point of contention between Somerville and Cambridge. The Russell farm on Broadway, known for its agricultural productivity in the early days of the town, also served as a roadside inn for other farmers on their way to Boston. Built in the mid-1700s with an addition at the turn of the nineteenth century, the house and farm were still active when Irving L. Russell, a market gardener, was cultivating the remaining forty acres in 1886. As the ancestral land was gradually sold off, John Medina, the Boston hair stylist, was one of the new suburban businessmen to settle in the area. His elaborate garden and greenhouse on part of the Russell estate at the corner of Broadway and Curtis Street became a neighborhood landmark before he relocated in 1887 to the Medina Building in Davis Square. By 1898, Chief James Hopkins of the Somerville Fire Department was lamenting the loss of the ancient farmhouse, blaming its destruction on a fire set by arsonists.

If anyone mentioned "blasting" in West Somerville during 1895, that person had to be prepared for more than a heated discussion. The City of Cambridge owned a portion of valuable ledge on Clarendon Hill within the boundary of Somerville. Since the time of separation from Charlestown, the area had been subjected to violence as the rock was ripped from the quarry and carried away for building purposes. When the needs of construction increased, so did the activity at the ledge, culminating in the daily use of dynamite to blast rock. The Clarendon Improvement Society demanded public hearings in order to put an end to the bone-rattling explosions. According to the many people who filled the Aldermanic Chambers on August 14, the excavation, which was a hundred feet deep, was being enlarged on a weekly basis. Located close to the line between Cambridge and Somerville, the ledge had experienced so many blasts that the foundations of nearby houses had been weakened, plaster had dropped from walls, large quantities of crockery were broken and nervous women had been rendered prostrate for weeks at a time. Besides being a hazard to children in the neighborhood, the nuisance was causing property values to plummet.

Under the glare of the public spotlight, it emerged that Cambridge did not have and had not applied for a permit to do the work. The firm of Collins and Ham had been hired by Cambridge without going through any dealings with the Somerville government. The company was denied a license in 1895, much to the annoyance of Cambridge. In an effort to start work again, Collins and Ham provided the Somerville politicians with a trial run of "modified blasting," which was supposed to be harmless to the neighborhood. Unconvinced, Somerville denied the company a license in 1896, yet continued the hearings.

For years, the patience of those on Clarendon Hill was strained as Cambridge exerted pressure to have the blasting resume. One sufferer, John T. Rafferty of 16 Clarendon Street, decided to take matters into his own hands. On the night of May 11, 1898, Rafferty assaulted an alderman in front of Somerville City Hall. Coming from the Clarendon Hill district himself, John Cummings of Holland Street had stated publicly that he had signed a paper in favor of Collins and Ham. Rafferty began by calling Cummings a "rogue." Cummings made the mistake of shaking his finger at the volatile Irishman and shouting, "I am free to do as I please!" Infuriated, Rafferty attacked, leaving Cummings senseless and bleeding on the concrete steps. While Cummings was carried to his home, Rafferty was held on a charge of assault, and the hearing went on for several hours. By 1903, Collins and Ham were still petitioning for blasting rights even after their petition to the state legislature had been refused.

The real estate agents in West Somerville blessed the day that overhead wires and double tracks for the electric trolleys were being installed along Clarendon Hill in 1895. Not only would this facilitate the commute to Boston and open up the neighborhood to development, but it would also necessitate the removal of five hundred West End Railway employees from in town to the top of the hill. Many of the railway drivers and mechanics preferred living nearby in West Somerville.

One such was motorman number 7017, John Byrnes, who ran a car from the enormous Clarendon Hill car stables. Born in Ireland, Byrnes had come to America in 1852. He first drove a coach from Porter's Hotel in Cambridge to Scollay Square. When the Somerville Horse Railroad succeeded the coaches, he could be found on the front platform of a car, driving salespeople and merchants over to Charlestown and Boston. During the Civil War, he enlisted in the Somerville Company E of the Thirty-ninth Massachusetts Regiment, serving honorably for three years. Upon his return, he continued his work for the Boston Elevated Railway. He was described in an 1898 interview with the *Globe* as "bluff, hale and hearty. His pathway through sunshine and storm, through the heat of summers and the blizzards of winters, has been one of constant geniality."

Despite the transition from farmland to car barn use, the Clarendon Hill property owned by the Boston Elevated Railway was not only given to operating lines that radiated from the hilltop. For several years, over five acres of company land were dedicated to the use of gardens for motormen. In 1907, several "knights of the soil" of different ethnic backgrounds tilled their own vegetable plots. When not on duty, they would don overalls and big-brimmed hats as they raised sweet corn, potatoes, cabbages, tomatoes and several strains of beans. The most renowned was Joe Vello, a railway veteran of forty years, whose plot was admired by his co-workers: Thomas Rennie, James Fitzgerald, E.R. Ogier and John McCarthy. It was an unconsciously astute move on the part of the company to ingratiate itself with the Clarendon Hill community and also to facilitate a harmonious work environment for its employees.

BUILDING ONE FOR THE HOME TEAM

In 1908, the city spent $1,500 laying out and grading a new athletic field on land formerly known as the Wild Cat Hill gravel pit. The area of about three and a half acres was bounded by Powder House Boulevard and Alewife Brook Parkway. Originally, the recreational field was to include areas for baseball, basketball, tennis, cricket, croquet, a playfield for children, an outdoor gymnasium, running track, swimming pool and boating and skating on the brook, as well as a grandstand and field house. The "new "Somerville Field" (now the site of Dilboy Stadium) was very popular with the various clubs and athletic teams, and a number of outside school teams made use of the field, bringing income to the city. Amateur sports now had a home.

Within a few years, Somerville's own Charles Taylor would build Fenway Park, a splendid home for our nation's favorite pastime. Born in Charlestown, Taylor learned the printer's trade at the *Boston Traveler*, and at the age of only sixteen he enlisted in the Union army during the Civil War. Wounded in 1863, Taylor returned home and took employment as a reporter and correspondent for the *New York Tribune*. In 1866, Taylor married Georgianna Davis, and the couple enjoyed a beautiful home on Spring Hill.

In 1872, led by retail giant Eben Jordan (founder of Jordan Marsh), six prominent Boston businessmen invested $150,000 in a new city newspaper. The *Boston Globe* debuted on March 4, 1872, but the paper faltered financially in its first year. Jordan turned to Taylor as the paper's first business manager. Due to his financial skills, Taylor was made a partner and president. Charles Taylor was recognized not only as a great editor, but was also among the greatest newspaper managers of his day. He would eventually bring all three of his sons into the paper. In fact, a member of the Taylor family would serve as publisher of the *Boston Globe* for the next 125 years. In 1997, Benjamin B. Taylor, a great-grandson of General Taylor, became the fifth and final member of the family to serve as publisher.

At the age of fifty-eight, General Taylor purchased a baseball team for his son John. The team, formerly owned by Charles Somers, one of the principal founders of the American Baseball League, was known at various times as the Puritans, Pilgrims, the Plymouth Rocks and, in 1908, the Boston Red Sox.

Charles H. Taylor, Somerville businessman and earlier publisher and editor of the *Boston Globe*.

In the early days, the team played ball at the Huntington Avenue grounds, now part of Northeastern University. In 1910, tired of his leasing arrangement, Taylor announced plans to build a state-of-the-art ballpark—Fenway Park—for his Red Sox. The park's peculiar dimensions were built to keep nonpaying customers out.

Fenway Park, ca. 1914. *Library of Congress's Prints and Photograph Division.*

Fenway Park hosted its first professional baseball game on April 20, 1912. The Red Sox defeated the New York Highlanders, later known as the Yankees, before twenty-seven thousand fans, seven to six in eleven innings. The press took little note of the event, however, due to the sinking of the *Titanic* only days before. Fenway also lost out on hosting the amazing 1915 World Series. The series attracted over forty-two thousand fans and the game was held at Braves Field to accommodate the overwhelming crowds. No matter, the Boston Red Sox defeated the Philadelphia Phillies four games to one.

BASEBALL HEROES

According to his sister, Lawrence "Lolly" Gatto was a handsome young man, with blond wavy hair and blue eyes. One of nine children, Lolly had an extroverted personality and was "always telling jokes which had the whole family laughing." Lawrence was the leading hitter on Somerville High's championship team of 1941, hitting .425 for the season. The team won the championship with an amazing nineteen wins in twenty starts. Ernest Morrison, in his book *Play ball!*, wrote that "Lawrence's greatest joy was playing baseball at Somerville High School…He excelled at it and already was being scouted by the Boston Red Sox and others." Barney Curtin, his coach at the time, considered Larry "a good bet to become a major leaguer!"

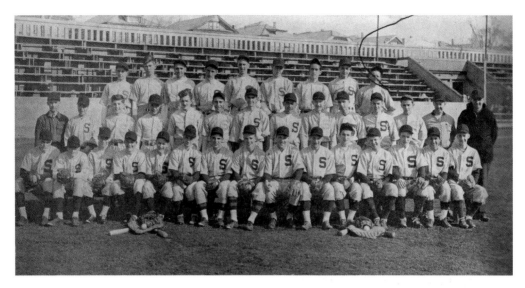

Lawrence "Lolly" Gatto was the leading hitter on the Somerville High School championship team. Lolly is in the bottom row, sixth from the left. The Radiator *(Yearbook), 1941.*

Lawrence Gatto was killed when his troop's ship was torpedoed and sunk in November 1943. Lawrence was a radio operator and was on his way to Africa to serve in the Army Corps.

Other great Somerville ball players included Harold Pie Traynor, a member of the Baseball Hall of Fame; Frank Shanty Hogan and Arthur "Skinny" Graham, from Magoun Square, who played for the Boston Red Sox in the 1930s; and John J. "Leftie" Murphy, who was killed by a sniper's bullet at the battle of Bougainville. The John J. Murphy Playground was dedicated at Foss Park on September 11, 1998.

Chapter 9

Quarry and Walnut Tree Hills

BECOMING INVENTIVE

The Revolution Set in Stone

Somehow the powder house endured when so many reminders of the past were subject to the unrelenting drive to develop, improve and modernize. The old round tower built from the stone of Quarry Hill itself was originally constructed for a very practical purpose: it was a windmill. Its creator was John Mallet, a French Huguenot and a shipwright turned miller who had first settled in Worcester County. Coming to Charlestown to escape difficulties with the native tribes, he bought land in 1704 and proceeded to put together his mill on the edge of a quarry. Wide blades surmounted the conical mill top and caught the wind, thus turning the heavy grinding stones. Mallet's business sense was sound, and the mill produced a profit as well as grain.

Michael Mallet, the son, inherited the family business in 1720, yet for reasons unknown, he sold it to the Massachusetts Bay Colony in 1747. Not interested in grinding meal, the colony leaders were determined to use the structure for gunpowder storage. By 1774, it was evident that the possibility of clashing with the British was becoming increasingly likely and that the powder magazine was indeed a valuable asset. For their part, the English decided that 250 barrels of gunpowder and other munitions stored by restless colonists could not be tolerated.

In an unexpected move, British troops rowed from Boston to Ten Hills Farm, successfully penetrated the Charlestown interior and removed much of the contents of the powder house. Public reaction was swift as locals planned retaliation. It was not yet time for them to act, so discretion supplanted valor, and they removed the remaining supplies farther inland before the English could strike again. Although still used as a magazine during the siege of Boston, the powder house building was turning into an antique.

The land, ledge and tower came into the possession of the Tufts family in 1818. This branch of the prolific Tufts tree, namely Peter Tufts, farmed tree acres for decades. Fortunately, the powder house itself was left undisturbed, overlooking a meandering meadow stream called "Two Penny Brook." Gradually, legends attached themselves to the picturesque structure. The most romantic involved a beautiful Arcadian maiden

Powder house, 1935. *Historic American Buildings Survey, Arthur C. Haskell, photographer. Library of Congress, Prints and Photographs Division.*

who fled from a cruel and abusive master. She took refuge with the powder house miller but was pursued by the evil farmer, who smooth talked his way into gaining access to her hiding place. Justice prevailed. Just as the evildoer reached for the girl, he plunged to his death under the heavy wheels of the mill. The maiden escaped unharmed. The powder house, in silence, continued to keep watch over the neighborhood as the farm was handed on to generations of Tufts.

A Park for the People

The city of Somerville soon learned that preservation often included dramatic changes. When the Nathan Tufts heirs donated land around the old powder house for use as a public park (1893), the neighbors on Quarry Hill rejoiced. They did not anticipate the makeover that the area would undergo. A local writer complained that "it looks as if the old relic of the revolutionary days [the powder house] had been moved bodily and set up in a new location." The root of concern involved a radical modernization of the hill.

City teams of about thirty men were employed in laying out new roadways, grading, filling and leveling. Workers cleaned the ledge area, removing overgrown bushes and unwanted trees. Along the stone edge, a parapet wall was constructed in order to prevent

Powder House Terrace construction. *Somerville Annual Report, 1902.*

children from hurting themselves in a fall. The muddy land at the base was filled in. In earlier times, the Emerson pickle factory operating nearby had used the site as a dumping ground for vegetable waste and rusting metal cans. Because builders were greatly interested in constructing ample homes for the middle class just outside of Davis Square, this improvement was greeted with great enthusiasm.

The powder house itself underwent a major face-lift. The city was determined to improve upon the original structure by changing the doorway to the side opposite the original opening. Much more "important," the new door was framed by large blocks of Medford granite. A greatly enlarged window was inserted in order to allow in more light. New iron grilles defined, as well as protected, the new additions. A new flagpole was put up as a finishing touch. Victorian sensibilities were greatly satisfied by the toning up of the old relic. They thoroughly enjoyed the charms of antiquity, but were determined to set their own stamp on legend and history.

"LIGHT ON A HILL"

Before Charles Tufts's gift of land became Tufts College, Walnut Hill had long been stripped of the trees that once covered it. Revolutionary War soldiers (Hessians) and shipbuilders from neighboring Medford had deforested it for their own use. Yet by 1898, the summit once more was being cultivated with a rich variety of trees.

The institution had been chartered in 1852 as the end result of a movement by well-known Universalists to establish a college with a religious focus. It formally opened in 1855, with the first handful of students graduating in 1857. Straddling both Somerville and Medford, the university maintained strong contacts with both communities. A late nineteenth-century guidebook extolled the panoramic view from the steps of the reservoir that used to dominate the hill off Packard Avenue. The spectator could enjoy a scene

> embracing the tidal flats of the Mystic River, Malden, Medford, the thick woods of the Middlesex Fells, Winchester, Arlington, Cambridge, the Brookline hills, Somerville, and in the far southeast, the Blue Hills. Here, too, are to be seen especially beautiful sunsets.

The terraced hillside was a bucolic setting for Ballou Hall, named in honor of Reverend Hosea Ballou, the first president of the college. Nearby, Goddard Chapel featured a hundred-foot campanile that was a landmark to the Somervillians who lived in Davis Square. This building was especially theirs since it was constructed from some of the stone of Quarry Hill.

Another part of the old campus was dedicated to the Museum of Natural History, having been built and endowed by the famous showman Phineas T. Barnum. Barnum, more spectacularly known as a collector and exhibitor of the bizarre, was an ardent Universalist who did not hesitate to publish his beliefs in a pamphlet. He was ideal for the institution because he contributed generously to the college but did not attend any

Students take time out from studying at Ballou Hall, Tufts College, 1853. Gleason's Pictorial Drawing Room Companion. *Courtesy of the Somerville Public Library.*

Tufts graduates, class of 1870. *From* Here and There at Tufts, *1907.*

of the trustee meetings. His gift of Jumbo the Elephant's hide to the museum provided countless numbers of students with a good luck charm. They would touch or tug upon the stuffed pachyderm's tail in order to guarantee success in upcoming exams. Time took its toll on Jumbo, finally culminating in his final destruction in a blaze.

The 1898 description of the delightful campus continued with mention of the pump that yielded excellent spring water. Near the library, it quenched the thirst of the students in West and East Dormitory Halls. Other college buildings recognized the achievements of prominent Unitarians, such as Paige Hall, which honored Reverend Lucius Paige, the tireless city clerk of Cambridge who combined his ministry with civic service. When the school became coeducational in 1892, Metcalf Hall on Professors' Row housed some of the women who used the well-worn footpath to cross the broad fields of the college to Broadway near the old powder house.

At this time, the college estate contained about one hundred acres. It prided itself on its broad array of courses: liberal arts, physics, chemistry and the technical work of the engineering department, which was housed in the Bromfield-Pearson School on College Avenue. Of particular pride was the Divinity School (1869) and a Medical School (1893).

THE OTHER INVENTOR OF THE TELEPHONE

Before becoming professor of physics at Tufts in 1874, Amos E. Dolbear (1837–1910) had already experienced enough of life to satisfy many Victorians. Born in Connecticut, he moved to Worcester by the time he was sixteen in order to apprentice in a pistol factory. He kept changing direction. He taught school in Missouri, worked in the armory at Springfield, Massachusetts, and then labored in a machine shop in Taunton. Nothing seemed to satisfy him for very long.

The 1860s found him at Ohio Wesleyan University, where he supported himself by teaching music and organ. Before graduating in 1866, he had constructed a "talking telegraph" and a receiver with a permanent magnet combined with a thin metal diaphragm that would anticipate later work on the telephone. He obtained an advanced degree, taught in Bethany College, West Virginia, and, for one brief year, was mayor of the town. It was time to move on again.

By 1874, he had settled on Professors' Row at the corner of Curtis Street. Characteristically, he kept very busy with his college workload while preparing a book for publication. In an 1876 statement to the American Academy of Arts and Sciences, he proclaimed that he was continuing work in telephony, some of which dated back to 1865. However, his courses demanded his attention and his assistant was available only part time at best. Meanwhile, Alexander Graham Bell was busily experimenting.

A mutual friend of both Bell and Dolbear, Percival Richards of Medford assured the Tufts teacher that Bell's tests were in the early stages. Dolbear falsely assumed that he still had plenty of time to work, but, unfortunately, this was not the case. In 1876, Bell filed his application for his groundbreaking invention, only hours ahead of Elisha Gray, another inventor with a similar concept. By March, Bell's patent was a reality much to

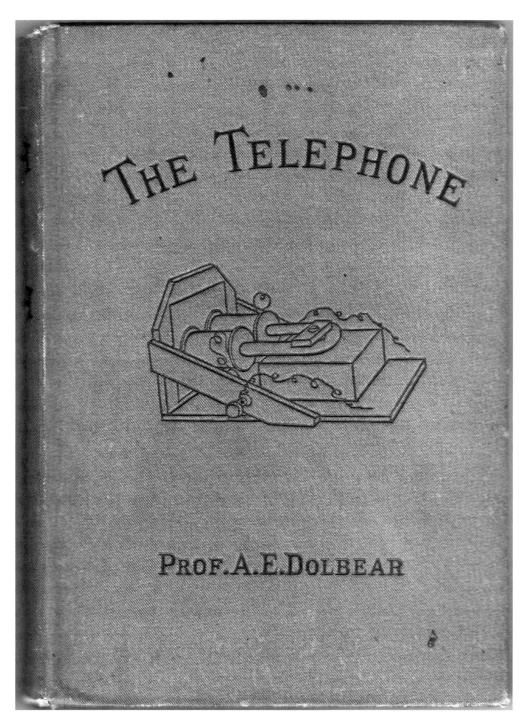

The Telephone by Amos Emerson Dolbear (Lea and Shepard, 1877). Published one year after Alexander Graham Bell's patent, Dolbear tells his own story of his telephone work.

the chagrin of Dolbear, who commented that he had relied on Richard's perceptions without questioning them. The fact that Dolbear was limited to the help of a part-time assistant and could only work some evenings and weekends did not ease the situation. Disheartened, he said, "I suppose that I shall lose both the honor and profit of the invention." Most inventors would have given up, but Dolbear was tenacious.

Dolbear filed his own telephone patent application in 1876 and started to collaborate with the Western Union Company. At the same time, Bell founded American Bell Telephone Company and was suing Dolbear and others for patent infringement. There was an out-of-court settlement, despite Western Union's claim that Bell had not produced a "working" telephone. The patents of Dolbear, Elisha Gray and Thomas Edison, who had also entered the fray, became the property of American Bell.

Still teaching, Dolbear then incorporated the Dolbear Electric Telephone Company, having obtained a patent for a telephone receiver in April 1881. Bell countered with a lawsuit and, of course, won. In an appeal to the Supreme Court, Dolbear lost again. He turned his attention to wireless.

This time, his invention depended on phones grounded by metal rods driven into the earth. He was able to communicate sound over half a mile, thus anticipating the work of Guglielmo Marconi. The general public still thought that most experimentation with electricity would never amount to anything more than a gimmick. Dolbear decided to get a patent for his device but not to pursue it actively. He was granted a patent for a wireless telegraph in 1882, with an improvement on the device in 1886.

At the turn of the new century, Marconi was ready to bring his wireless telegraph to America. Because of Dolbear's patents, the Italian had to buy him out in order to operate the Marconi Company in the United States. The *Boston Globe* printed accounts of the Marconi/Dolbear controversy, but no lasting recognition came to the local academic. Undaunted, he continued to push scientific boundaries.

At last, in 1897, he was recognized for something completely different, namely his work with insects. He had noticed over time the correlation between temperature and the rapidity of crickets' chirping. Summers on Walnut Hill had taught him to listen as their sounds filled the drowsy air. When he catalogued his observations, he realized that the insect noises were not random: increasing warmth produced increasingly faster cricket sounds. His scientific formula describing the phenomenon became known as Dolbear's Law, or the cricket as thermometer. Undisputed fame had at last come to the professor.

Known as "Dolly" to his students, Amos Dolbear was an extraordinary, devoted member of the Tufts faculty. For several decades, his expertise prepared young men to follow their scientific dreams. His own son, Clinton E. Dolbear, became an inventor and staunch defender of his father's work. About the same age as Marconi, he commented that the European inventor was only eight when the senior Dolbear was already experimenting with the wireless telegraph. Even the *Scientific American* (1881) remarked that if Dolbear's phone had been produced in a more timely fashion, the Tufts professor might have been credited with the invention.

Also far-reaching was his unconditional support of the college's decision to admit women in 1892. He was in the minority of the faculty to do so, but facing opposition was just a familiar part of taking a stand. He had spent a good many years in combat himself.

Dolbear was a prolific inventor whose work was not fully recognized in his own day. His unquenchable spirit, however, could not be challenged. The 1903 *Somerville Journal* reported that "outwardly the years may leave traces [on Dolbear], but his youthful heart and cheering words make him a welcome friend among the students, all of whom love him."

BELL'S SOMERVILLE CONNECTION

It was 1871 when the twenty-four-year-old Alexander Graham Bell (1847–1922) was hired at the Boston School for Deaf Mutes, where he instructed deaf children by using his father's program of visible speech. His preference for speech over sign language evoked both praise and condemnation. Expanding his horizon, he opened his own short-lived school in 1872. By 1873, Bell had joined the faculty of Boston University's School of Oratory and was trying experiments with the multiple telegraph.

Bell made a very fortunate decision when he accepted Mabel Hubbard as one of his private pupils. Mabel had become deaf as a result of a childhood case of scarlet fever. Gardiner Greene Hubbard, her father, a wealthy lawyer, wanted his daughter to speak with clarity and ease. Although she was ten years younger than her teacher, Mabel and Bell quickly became friends and then formed an attachment. Mr. Hubbard would not allow the marriage until Bell was more financially secure. Bell worked more intensely on what he called his "harmonic telegraph." Hubbard decided to invest in his future son-in-law's experiments. His money came from his extensive real estate holdings in Boston and his successful investments during the Civil War. Hubbard's fortune would be crucial to Bell's success in later years.

By 1875, Bell was setting up a workshop at 109 Court Street, the site of the telegraph manufactory of Charles Williams of Somerville. Williams had already supplied parts and apparatus to Thomas Edison, as well as renting him space. It was natural for Williams to let the young Boston University professor put together a lab on the top floor of his building. Plus, Williams had an employee named Thomas Watson, a brilliant young mechanic, who might be a suitable assistant for Bell. Williams could not have known how completely perfect his choice would be. On the personal front, Bell became engaged to Mabel while entering into a formal business partnership with her father.

The Bell/Watson team focused on sending speech over a wire. On June 2, 1875, they were successful in transmitting an unintentional "twang" from a transmitter in one room to a receiver located in another. Working very long hours, much to the dismay of Mabel, Bell and Watson forged ahead. In 1876, everything fell into place, especially in March, when a patent was granted for the phone and the famous message, "Mr. Watson, come here, I want you," had been delivered. Knowing that he had to get his invention before the public, he displayed the phone at the Centennial Exposition in Philadelphia and then, with the help of Watson, traveled to several New England cities in order to demonstrate the new instrument. He was greeted with mild enthusiasm.

Charles Williams did not doubt that the telephone was going to amount to something. In early 1877, he negotiated with Bell and Hubbard to be the sole manufacturer of telephones for general use and to get commission on any that he leased. By April, Williams also decided that it would be enormously convenient for his own business, and so the world's first outdoor telephone line was opened between his shop and his home at the corner of Arlington and Lincoln Streets, Somerville. Word of the curious new device spread so rapidly that the Williams manufactory was crowded with visitors who wanted to talk with Mrs. Williams and others at the house. Williams was assigned telephone numbers 1 and 2. There was no charge for the service.

As 1877 progressed, Bell and Mabel were married and a new search for additional phone users was on. Charles Williams suggested that some Somerville friends, the Downers of 170 Central Street, might be willing to take a risk on the new contraption. When approached, Cutler Downer, the chief banker at Stone and Downer, State Street, did not want to have anything to do with the "toy" and refused to invest any money in its development. He declared that he had seen too many gimmicks come and go. However, his sons, Roswell and Frank, who were also in banking, were willing take a fling on the new technology. They were leased phone numbers 3 and 4, thus becoming the first to install commercial telephones. In a testimonial written to Gardiner Hubbard in May 1877, they stated that phones had been connected between their State Street offices and their home in North Somerville. Their testimonies would be used in future advertising.

We have used them constantly since with good success; in fact, we have become so used to them, that we use them in preference to the Morse [code] system, being able to transmit our messages much faster, and with a great deal less labor. We have experimented several times with musical instruments…the playing of the piano being heard very distinctly… We can certainly endorse the telephone…and believe that it can be used practically.

Cutler Downer still thought that the telephone was not a respectable machine to have in a business setting. Though he wanted the bank phone to be hidden from public view, he did concede that it might be interesting for recreational use. Roswell was successful in having the phone installed in a small room on the second floor of his Somerville house and even having the line extended and connected to 177 Central Street, where Maria L. Brown, a family friend, lived. The two households could now chat. But Roswell was responsible for paying the phone leases since he was the enthusiast.

Undaunted, he arranged for Bell to come out to Somerville to demonstrate the phone at the home of Gershom Burnham of Sycamore Street. The neighbors were invited to talk to one another on the two instruments that were installed in two separate rooms. It was a wildly entertaining evening, but no one signed up to lease the invention. Bell was rather discouraged. He was convinced that Williams should step up production. Williams obliged, manufacturing all the phones in the world with the help of two assistants. Bell and Watson continued their research and development, waiting for the

Charles Williams Jr., of Arlington Street, owned the electrical shop in Boston where the Bell telephone was created.

phone to catch on. Suddenly, in the early summer of 1877, there was an urgent demand for instruments. Hubbard could not afford to give the business more money. Writing to the board of directors of the infant Bell Telephone Company, he begged for an advance for Williams:

He has been making for the last 10 days, 25 phones a day. This is not enough to supply even the present demands and he has, therefore, agreed to manufacture 40 small, 10 box and 10 of magneto cells a day if he can receive a further $1,000.

By 1879, Williams's business did not have the manpower or physical capacity to keep up with the phone surge. As other makers were licensed, his work was considered the model for the new industry. Inadvertently, he was the person who received the first payment of a telephone bill. In his cash book, he recorded that he had accepted twenty dollars from J. Emory Jr. of Charlestown for the installation of a telephone connecting his house to his brother's across the street. Not knowing what to do with the money, Williams carried it in his pocket for over a week until he could check in with Bell.

THE WRENCH WIZARD

Somerville's neighborhoods were filled with inventors. Daniel Stillson (1826–1900), a machinist by trade, came from New Hampshire to enlist in the Union navy during the Civil War. Serving as a fireman on the steamer *R.B. Forbes*, he impressed his commanding officer, Colonel Levi Greene, with his unique mechanical inventiveness. After the war, Greene was recruited by the Walworth Company, systems and valve manufacturers located in Boston and Cambridgeport. Dan Stillson applied for a job with his old navy comrade. He was hired immediately.

By 1869, Stillson had designed a wooden model of an adjustable wrench that would do away with the multiple ones used every day by mechanics. The Walworth people examined his model and ordered him to create one in steel. When put to the test, the prototype successfully twisted off a length of pipe while leaving the wrench intact. Not only were they delighted, but they could foresee that the tool could revolutionize the pipe industry.

Colonel Greene and the executives insisted that Stillson obtain a patent in his own name. In return for exclusive production rights, the company would provide him with all the necessary legal advice and pay any fees. The astonished Stillson agreed. Over the course of his lifetime, he earned over $70,000 while the Walworth Company profited enormously from manufacturing a wrench that became a staple in every mechanic's toolbox.

Having built his own home at 55 Tennyson Street, Stillson settled down with his family, served as an alderman and became a vital member of the building committee of the "new" library on Central Hill. Stillson was a prime example of the self-educated, skillful artisan who searched out Somerville as his residence of choice.

Daniel C. Stillson, Civil War veteran, patented an adjustable wrench in 1876, making life easier for the workingman.

Somerville's Submariner

While constructing a sewer outlet in the Belfast, Maine harbor in 1902, Irving M. Cottrell became intrigued with working underwater. Although he had no professional training or experience, he strapped on a cumbersome diving outfit, plunged into the ocean and proceeded to lay the first of several hundred feet of cast-iron pipe. Cottrell was lauded as an instant expert because of the very fact that few men would dare to take on such dangerous exploits.

Opportunity came his way when he was offered a job as superintendent of a maritime railway in East Boston. He relocated his family to Somerville because it was affordable. The Cottrells found a comfortable home on Highland Avenue, thus ensuring that his commute to and from the city would be short.

Necessity almost demanded that Cottrell become an inventor. His job involved handling explosives in Boston Harbor and finding bodies of crime victims who had been dumped into the water. Since danger was at every turn, his thoughts focused on ways of eliminating risk. As he had done before, he took charge and methodically developed equipment. First, he designed safety improvements for his diving outfit. Then he tackled the difficulty of reclaiming heavy objects. His hard work paid off when he invented a machine that would help raise submerged vessels. By 1910, he described himself filled with great hope that he could invent something of significance. There were unsuccessful attempts. Finally, in 1928, Cottrell achieved his ultimate goal. He created a mechanism that would rescue men imprisoned in a sunken submarine.

Irving Cottrell did not gain national recognition for his efforts. He rated a few articles in the *Somerville Journal,* and was acknowledged locally. It was enough for him to know that he had saved a few lives.

THE EFFICIENCY EXPERT

As Somerville moved rapidly from an agrarian to an industrial society, quick-thinking inventors turned from improving farm equipment to engaging in designing machines that would be faster, easier to run and more profitable. The middle class firmly believed that the individual could make a difference.

Erastus Woodward, a mechanical engineer, was all about motion. Working from his home on Wigglesworth Street, he pumped out an array of patents that focused on streamlining repetitive movements. He started with a variation on the mechanized sewing machine, whereby buttons could be rapidly attached to cloth. Moving on to transportation, he worked with Joseph Millet of Charlestown to improve the starting of railroad cars and other carriages. Their design of 1868 offered car operators the benefit of greater leverage and the use of antifriction rollers. Woodward's fastening-driving machine, perfected in the 1880s, allowed the mechanic to control the motion of the jack by one treadle, while stopping and starting the process with a second treadle. His nail-loading gun could secure nails on shoe heels faster than a cobbler could do it. Finally, after observing the tedious hand stamping of letters performed by post office clerks, he invented a marking machine that processed mail efficiently. Very much ahead of his time, Woodward was a one-man research and development company.

Chapter 10

Strawberry Hill and Davis Square

BECOMING PERFECT

EXTRAORDINARY YEOMAN

Originally, the Timothy Tufts (1735–1805) property embraced 160 acres of pasture and farmland. The ancestral farmhouse, anchoring the corner of Elm and Willow Streets, was built about a year before hostilities with the English began. The house was meant to last. In the opening days of the Revolution, it bore witness to the march of the British troops on the road to Lexington and Concord in 1775. Stopping to drink at the

Timothy Tufts House, Willow and Elm Streets, 1894. Timothy Tufts was a farmer, mechanical genius and holder of several patents. *Courtesy of Maynard and Laverne Batchelder.*

farm pump, the redcoats created such a stir that the Tuftses' dog barked out a patriotic warning to the sleeping family. From behind the front-room curtains, the startled parents and children watched the soldiers rush to their fateful clash with the minutemen. Timothy quickly dressed and went through the neighborhood alerting the residents.

Hours later, the defeated soldiers were retreating with the colonists in pursuit. Other Patriots waited for the exhausted British, while on the ridge behind the farmhouse, a cannon was planted on the high ground. A murderous fire ensued, cutting down several of the uniformed soldiers. Realizing that they were in mortal danger, the redcoats picked up their pace and rushed by the Tuftses' yard. When all was safe, the ever-practical Timothy buried the dead in a portion of his garden near Willow Avenue. Always spoken of as Timothy Tufts, Esquire, he was chosen as a selectman from most of 1780–92.

The Renaissance Farmer

Before the next Timothy Tufts (1818–1910) was born, his birthplace had already been a historical icon to generations of Somerville citizens. When he reached adulthood in the 1840s, he became aware that some of the clay-rich soil on the farm had more potential than just being used for pastureland. He organized the Tufts Brick Manufactory, realizing that he needed to produce excellent bricks in a timely fashion. Like his relatives before him, he took matters into his own hands by inventing a brick-making machine that would solve the problem. According to a highly complimentary story in the *Somerville Journal*, the Tufts brickyard could turn out over a hundred thousand bricks per year. The *New York Times* saw fit to comment that his invention had netted him $50,000.

When Somerville men were called to defend the Union in 1861, Timothy Tufts was approaching middle age, yet he wanted to do his part. As the Civil War continued, he stepped up work on his latest invention. His best effort was an experimental repeating cannon of his own design. The rapid-fire gun could release eighty-five shots per minute and would be of enormous use to the Union side. Without hesitation, he traveled to Washington with his weapon in hopes of showing it to President Lincoln.

Unfortunately, Lincoln was not available to meet with the Somerville brick maker. As Tufts stood beside his cannon on Pennsylvania Avenue, General Banks, another Massachusetts native, happened by. Banks was impressed with the gun and urged Tufts to obtain financial backing so that it could be put into production. Elated, Tufts returned home with his weapon. With due diligence, he contacted the wealthy investor who had advanced him the money to have the prototype built. He also approached a Waltham factory that agreed to begin manufacturing as soon as the money was secured. All seemed promising until the investor contracted typhoid fever and, in a fit of derangement, drowned himself. The project was aborted. Tufts resigned himself to firing his weapon during recruiting rallies on Prospect Hill. After the war, the gun was used in July Fourth celebrations.

Several years later, Tufts created a canker worm exterminator. This proved very successful. Encouraged, he turned his hand to making a labor-saving stove, but never produced it. Eerily similar to the cannon experience, his investor had committed suicide. By his sunset years, he decided to devote his time to his lifelong interest in birds.

Always having beautiful golden pheasants and other exotics on his property, he constructed an enormous aviary on the farm. This barn-like structure gave shelter to over one hundred birds of many species. Many stuffed specimens adorned his home. The extent of his collection attracted several Harvard professors, who made repeat visits to Willow Avenue in order to study his birds and consult with their owner. An ardent sportsman, Tufts enjoyed going on hunting trips until his last years. At age eighty-five, he was such a sure shot that he brought down three ducks with one barrel.

The extended Tufts family once owned more than a tenth part of Somerville land. At some social gatherings on Winter Hill, there would be a huge number of Tufts relatives in a group of sixty or more. Their prolific families spread out to settle in Charlestown, Somerville, Medford and Malden. As the country developed, the Tuftses' influence dispersed throughout New England.

GOLD FEVER

True W. Townsend got much more than he bargained for when he bought several acres of the Tufts estate on Willow Avenue between Fosket and Linden Streets. The land was an old pasture where cows had grazed amid large outcroppings of blue stone, an ideal material for foundations. Transforming the property into salable house lots would be a demanding but clear-cut process.

Townsend hired men to blast away at the ledge in order to flatten the landscape. The heavy stone pieces could be used on-site or carted off for other Townsend projects. It was all going according to schedule until one spring morning when the developer arrived at his property and discovered that some of the rock debris glittered in the sun. Filling his pockets with samples, he rushed to his Boston office and approached Channing Hazeltine, another real estate speculator. Hazeltine dabbled in Colorado mining interests and presented himself as an expert mineralogist. It was almost too perfect when Hazeltine pronounced the word: "Gold!"

The next day, an enthusiastic Hazeltine escorted Townsend to the state assayer, S.P. Sharples, who declared that the Somerville ore contained gold, silver and some copper. If the vein proved rich enough, it could produce over $200 per ton. Townsend was almost speechless as he and Hazeltine hastened to Willow Avenue to evaluate what riches lay there for the taking. But the word had been spread by others who had also seen the sparkle in the rocks.

In a very insightful article, the May 24, 1896 *Boston Globe* set the scene.

> *The rising sun gilded the top of the old powder house and struck down into the new mine, revealing a motley gathering of men, women and children which included the halt, the lame and the blind, all searching for evidence of the precious yellow metal.*

Crowd control became a necessity but did not really happen. Real estate men in their office topcoats jabbed at the outcroppings. Day laborers brought their dump carts and loaded up loose rocks. The children of the neighborhood had the best time as they swarmed all over the big hole, climbing almost to the top of the miniature cliff.

As the days passed, even the scholarly became involved. Students from Tufts College made their way to the site to scoop up samples for their mineralogy classes. Harvard undergrads came in groups to make field trials. Professors Symth and Shaler from Cambridge offered observations that gold and silver might exist in a Somerville quarry; however, it would not amount to much. A few local residents commented that Harvard and Tufts notables might not recognize gold if they tripped over it.

In mid-June, Hazeltine and Townsend were advertising the Somerville Gold and Silver Mining Company, offering the public an opportunity to buy shares at the bargain price of ten cents each. Only a hundred thousand shares were to be sold at this rate. Besides, it was seen as a civic duty to invest.

> We anticipate that this [stock] will be taken at once by Somerville people who have the welfare of the city in mind, and who care to see determined by the shafting and tunneling the continuance of the rich ore found so near the surface which...promises to widen and grow richer still.

It was all wonderful until the gold- and silver-bearing quartz veins narrowed considerably. Processing the ore was not cost effective and news of the Somerville Bonanza began to disappear from the papers. After the first few months, people realized that the academics might have been on to something in their proclamation that the yield of precious metals would be modest. The mining company folded, having not completely reached its full complement of stockholders. The original plan of building on the site became the only sensible thing to do.

Life on Willow Avenue returned to the usual stuff of every day, including watching the cows in Carroll's pasture. The prediction seemed farfetched that the Somerville mine would be listed in the New York Stock Exchange and that, in a citywide celebration, six bartenders would be mixing drinks in the powder house. While it lasted, the bright promise of untold wealth had captured the imagination and energy of quite a few hardworking residents who just wanted the dream to be real.

DAVIS SQUARE—ON THE MOVE

Back in the day when there was nothing called Davis Square, the area was defined by multiple crossroads, dusty streets and a large trough where schoolboys such as H.L. Hovey watered travelers' horses. Weary travelers made their summer stop at Mrs. Hall's House (now the site of the West Somerville Library), a resort for lovers of good strawberries. "Hitch your horses and come in while I am having the berries picked," was her greeting, and the delay was never long, for she was prepared for business—a stroll

Postcard, Medina Building. This anchor building for Davis Square combined retail and apartments.

on the ledge, a short sniff among the wild roses and junipers and a seat at the table for the fragrant strawberries and cream.

Something of a square existed from 1871, going by several names or no name at all until 1883, when it officially became Davis Square. Its unofficial center was the hospitable home of Person Davis, a merchant and alderman in the first town government. Located at 255 Elm Street, opposite Chester, the house was gradually surrounded by commercial buildings—which was a sign of things to come.

By 1926, the house was standing empty amidst the confusion of the growing city. Mrs. Beatrice Carpenter, Davis's granddaughter, summed up the transformation: "Where once was an orchard now stands the Medina building, where gardens bloomed is the Lewis Block, and in front where there was a cherry tree, is now Worthylake's general store."

The Beauty Specialist

"Bangs have entirely gone out of style," said John Medina (1837–1924) of 485 Washington Street, Boston, to a *Globe* reporter. "Women now wear the sea-foam waves which are all the fashion." So spoke the oracle of beauty, a man from the Azores who would become one of the movers and shakers of Davis Square. Arriving in America as a young teen, John Medina spent a few years in Lawrence, where he focused on learning to speak English well enough to move easily in society. A natural artist, he trained to become a skilled hairdresser and manufacturer of hair goods. Before he was twenty, he

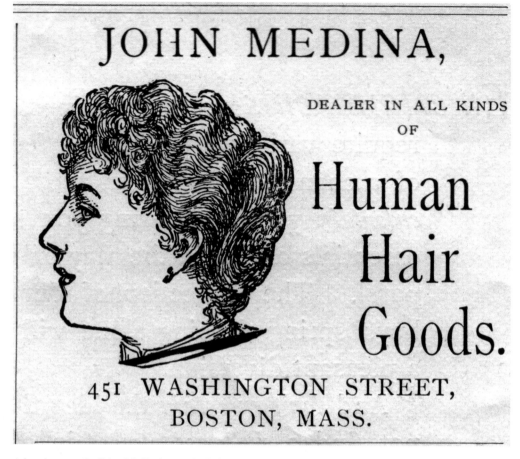

Advertisement for John Medina's swanky hair emporium, which also featured fancy face creams.

owned the wig-making establishment of Monsieur Chebasoll, a French stylist, who was known for his sophisticated beauty accessories. In just a few years, Medina opened up an elegant salon and hair supply palace in Worcester and then in Boston.

The Great Parisian Hair Store dazzled downtown Boston in the 1870s. Medina's major selling point was that he dealt only in pure human hair imported from Europe, not in imitations mixed with silk, jute or linen. These hybrid goods were sold at bargain prices, but were inferior and bound to disappoint. He advised that

> *it is not the fashion now to produce the impression of a great quantity of hair by a padding of other materials. Ladies wear a good braid or coil of false hair, exactly matching their own, but they do not load on, as formerly, an immense quantity of jute and other materials.*

Medina began to reach out in different business directions when he relocated to the up-and-coming suburb of Somerville. While still involved in his beauty salon, he joined forces with his brothers in an import/export company. Their small fleet of ships carried grain, lumber and passengers to the Azores. On the return trips, the three vessels were laden with more passengers and semitropical goods. In the meantime, Medina moved to Clarendon Hill, having purchased a house on a section of the Russell farm. Always improving his surroundings, he completely modernized the estate.

In 1887, Medina was being hailed as a pioneer in the revitalization of Davis Square. He erected the Medina Building, a handsome brick structure with his name on a plaque above the rounded front. Modern apartments, a bank and stores soon filled the building, creating an inviting place to stop while on the way to Tufts College, Powder House Square, Winter Hill, Medford, Cambridge or Arlington. It anchored the square, transforming the area into a destination rather than just a pass-through. Medina and his wife, Annie, liked the building so much that they moved into one of the new apartments.

Medina was often asked to run for office, but he declined the honor. One of his proudest civic moments was casting a vote for Abraham Lincoln, his first vote in America. Creating beauty was at the center of his life, whether it was expressed in his functional yet pleasing building or in his quality products designed to enhance the appearance. When talking about one of his specialties, Rico Cream, he summarized his very practical approach: "Beauty too often sacrifices to fashion. No face with a healthy complexion can be unattractive!" John Medina was a completely self-made man who always appreciated his customers and the place where he lived.

PEARSON'S PERFECT PICTURES

"I am experimenting upon an instrument which does for the eye what the phonograph does for the ear, which is the recording and reproduction of things in motion."
—Thomas A. Edison, 1888

Arthur G. Pearson was born in Boston in 1867 and moved to Somerville at the age of fifteen. Settling in the city, Arthur and his brother Fred opened a successful ice cream and candy store in the recently completed Odd Fellows Hall at 306 Broadway on Winter Hill.

Arthur married Otellia Stuber, daughter of a successful Philadelphia candy manufacturer. On her arrival in Somerville, Otellia became active in Christ Episcopal Church, the Somerville Heptorean Club and the Winter Hill Improvement Association. Arthur and Otellia had one daughter, Marguerite Stuber Pearson.

At the turn of the century, the Odd Fellows Lodge was in financial trouble. Local candy man Arthur Pearson had an idea for a "fun way to raise money"—open a movie theatre. In 1904, just eight years after Thomas Edison introduced the Vitascope, Pearson showed the first movie in Somerville. Using the large auditorium above his store, Pearson would call Somerville's first movie theatre Pearson's Perfect Pictures.

Pearson later recalled that the theatre opened with "fear and trembling."

Odd Fellows' Building on Broadway and Marshall Street, home of Pearson's Perfect Pictures and later the Winter Hill Theatre.

We started with a children's show one afternoon in October. The two pictures consumed about 10 minutes and illustrated songs about one half hour. The price was seven cents and each child got a bag of candy. The films [were] breaking every minute or so—the singers were so awful that it was ten days or so before we tried again. That show was good if short, we had a different machine, the very latest pictures, and the finest pianist we could secure…we soon found it necessary to run every night and Saturdays.

In the early days, short films were the norm. One of the first motion pictures ever copyrighted was a film showing Edison employee Fred Ott pretending to sneeze. Films got better and longer. The Massachusetts legislature passed the "Five Minute Law." The law required all picture houses to give patrons a five-minute recess every twenty minutes to relieve eyestrain.

In 1909, Pearson improved the theatre by adding an impressive pipe organ for live music. In 1922, he completed a major renovation and renamed it the Winter Hill Theatre. The Winter Hill Theatre remained open until 1927, when it succumbed to the competition from the seventeen-hundred-seat Capital Theatre directly across the street. Sadly, the Odd Fellows Hall was destroyed by fire on May 9, 1974.

Marguerite Stuber Pearson (1899–1978) grew up wanting to be a concert pianist, but in 1915, she contracted polio during a summer vacation in Maine and was confined to a wheelchair for the rest of her life. During her recovery, she took drawing lessons from illustrators Harold Anderson and Chase Emerson at the Fenway School of Illustration in Boston. Some of her earliest drawings were advertisements for her father's theatre.

She continued her studies at the Boston Museum School, studying privately with the famed artist and teacher Edmund C. Tarbell. Tarbell became so popular that his followers were called the "Tarbellites," known for their paintings of light-filled interiors, still lifes and figures. Upon seeing Marguerite's exhibition at the Guild of Boston Artists in 1931, Edmund Tarbell wrote to Pearson, "We are glad that you stick to the Boston tradition, and we look to you to uphold it, which you have more than done and are still doing." She worked as a magazine and news illustrator until turning to painting full time in 1922. By the mid-1940s, she had become quite financially successful. She belonged to many arts and artists groups, including the Guild of Boston Artists, the Rockport Art Association (where she moved in 1941), the American Artists Professional League and the New England Artists Group.

Many young Somerville women modeled for Marguerite, including Bertha Shaw, Ruth Walker, Hazel Hatfield, Marion Johnston, Irene Kelley, Dorothy Rankin, Marie Chambers and Mrs. S. Vincent Campelia. Marguerite also painted several Somerville mayors during her father's tenure as a city alderman from 1925 to 1933.

FIRST FAMILY OF MUSIC

The Hadleys were Somerville's first family of music. Coming from Boston in 1853, Samuel D. Hadley was appointed musical director of the town's few schools. His

Marguerite Pearson's self-portrait reveals her self-confidence. Print of original painting, oil on canvas. *Courtesy of the Somerville Public Library.*

The Somerville High School Orchestra. The Radiator *(Yearbook), 1895.*

sophisticated style amazed the children of brickyard workers as they listened to his oft-repeated motto: "Music is divided into three parts—rhythm, melody, and dynamics." A master of several instruments, he found joy in teaching, especially when the pupil was his own talented son.

Because S. Henry Hadley learned to love music when he was a small child, he knew that he wanted to follow in his father's footsteps. In 1862, he was one of six seniors graduating from Somerville High School. Just five years later, the young Hadley was hired as his father's assistant. He specialized in teaching grade schoolchildren to sight read, thus preparing the more advanced to join the high school orchestra. S. Henry Hadley's sons would build on family tradition by gaining nationwide attention.

Arthur, the younger boy, achieved recognition as lead cellist in the Boston Symphony Orchestra. Henry Hadley (1871–1937), the elder son, concentrated on bringing an American flavor to his music career. After staying in Europe, he conducted the Seattle Symphony and then became a founder of the San Francisco Symphony, followed by several productive years spent in composing five operas, numerous cantatas and many oratorios. Single-handedly, he shattered the prejudice in the United States toward American-born conductors leading symphony orchestras.

In 1937, Franklin D. Roosevelt paid tribute to the Somerville native, writing that "Henry Hadley's contributions to American music were rich and varied." This sincere compliment rather paled considering the rest of his accomplishments.

Henry Hadley united people and music by bringing them together in the Berkshire Festivals at Tanglewood. In order to provide his colleagues with a professional forum, he established the National Association for American Composers and Conductors. In 1926, he was responsible for the first synchronization of music with a feature film when he conducted the New York Philharmonic in playing the soundtrack for the movie *Don Juan* with John Barrymore. As homage to the teaching careers of his grandfather and father, he made a series of educational recordings that were a complete course in music appreciation geared toward the American public schools. It was only fitting that Tufts College, his alma mater, would honor him with the title of doctor of music.

HIP IN THE SQUARE

> *"If you really want to help the American theater, don't be an actress, dahling. Be an audience."*
> —*Tallulah Bankhead*

Until the 1870s, Davis Square was the home to farms and small estates. The arrival of the Arlington and Lexington branch of the Boston and Lowell Railroad brought businesses, people and their entertainments.

In 1914, Joseph Hobbs built the magnificent Somerville Theatre, designed by the firm of Funk and Wilcox of Boston. The building included a 1,200-seat theater, a bowling alley, billiard and pool room, a café and a 750-seat meeting hall with a dance floor. Originally decorated in a romantic style with pastel floral medallions, cherubs and red and gilt molded plaster, the theatre was later redone in the art deco style in the 1930s.

In 1926, the Hobbs family sold it to Arthur Viano. The Viano family owned the picture palace for almost sixty years. At one time, Somerville was home to fourteen theatres: Ball Square, Broadway, Capitol, Central, Day Street Olympia (E.M. Loews Davis Square), Highland, Orpheum, Pearson's Perfect Pictures, Somerville, Star, Strand, Teele Square, Union Square and Winter Hill.

In 1915, the Somerville Theatre Players stock company was formed. Members were recruited in New York at the end of each summer, with the season lasting nine months. Famed actors got their early start at the theatre, including Busby Berkeley, Kate Smith, Francis X. Bushman (*Ben Hur*) and Ray Bolger (best known as the scarecrow in *The Wizard of Oz*). One of the greatest drawing cards was the vaudeville cross-dressing act, Mr. Tommie Martell, known as the "pride of Somerville's heart." Martell played to sold-out houses as the lead female in the 1923 musical comedy, the *Fascinating Widow*.

In early 1919, a young New York actress, Tallulah Bankhead, came to West Somerville. On February 8, 1919, from her temporary home at the Woodbridge Hotel, Tallulah wrote to her beloved grandfather, John, about her experience in the company.

Postcard, Somerville Theatre, undated.

Somerville Theatre stock company, 1915–1916. *Courtesy of the Somerville Theatre Archives.*

Miss Estelle Winwood, English stage and movie actress and lifelong friend of Tallulah Bankhead. Theatre Magazine, *November 1918.*

Dear Grandfather: I know you will understand my not writing when I tell you all I have done…We opened Monday afternoon and I have made quite a hit in the show. I came up to stay two weeks and now they want me to stay on and play leads for the rest of the season but I can't possibly do it Granddaddy honey because I would be dead. We rehearse every morning from nine till twelve and then lunch, then a matinee every day, then dinner, then evening performances. I am nearly dead now and I have only been here a week. Then Somerville is a very large place as far as people go but no conveniences at all. I have a room in the only hotel here which is the tourist home. No private bath. I climb three flights of stairs. There is nothing here at all but I am working very hard for the experience…I wouldn't mind staying on for the experience but honey you don't know how hard it is…We are giving 12 performances a week…I can't wait to get back. I know something good will turn up. I hope so. Lots of love and kisses, Grandfather dear, my best friend. Tallulah

Tallulah Bankhead (1903–68) was born in Alabama, the daughter of Congressman William Bankhead. Her mother died of complications from childbirth and Tallulah was raised by her aunts and grandparents. After a few other minor roles in film and onstage, Tallulah went to England in 1923, where she became famous for her flamboyant personality and deep voice and was popular in the six plays in which she appeared. She returned to the United States and won acclaim for her later films: *The Little Foxes* (1939), *Skin of Our Teeth* (1942), Hitchcock's *Lifeboat* (1944) and Otto Preminger's *A Royal Scandal* (1948), as well as Noel Coward's *Private Lives* (1948). After her 1942 success, she bought a home in rural New York, where she lived at times with fellow actress Estelle Winwood, with whom she had a lifelong friendship. Tallulah was active in politics and campaigned for Franklin Roosevelt. Tallulah Bankhead retired from the stage in 1950. In 1952, she hosted for a television show, published her autobiography and starred in a nightclub act in Las Vegas. The Woodbridge Hotel, once considered a premier rental apartment, was located on College Avenue at the present site of Ciampa Manor. The hotel was destroyed in a series of devastating fires in 1979 and 1980.

The Somerville Theatre inherited the square's flamboyant past when hand organs with monkeys, hurdy-gurdies, harps and violins, dancing bears and German brass bands played in front of the homes and stores. Somervillians enjoyed their entertainments from behind and in front of the camera. Residents were featured in the "now missing" 1917 *The Message of the Glove*. According to historian David Guss, the film featured scenes from Patriot Day ceremonies on Prospect Hill and played for only one week at the Union Square Olympia.

Bibliography

Bacon, Edwin M. *Walks and Rides in the Country Round About Boston*. New York: Published for the Appalachian Mountain Club by Houghton Mifflin and Co., 1897.

Drake, Samuel Adams. *History of Middlesex County, Massachusetts*. Vols. 1 and 2. Boston: New England Historic Genealogical Society, 1879 and 1880.

Ellis, George. *Memoir of Luther V. Bell, M.D., LL.D.* Boston: Printed by J. Wilson and Sons, 1863.

Goodell, Abner Cheney. *Trial and Execution for Petit Treason, of Mark and Phillis*. Cambridge, MA: J. Wilson and Sons, 1883.

Haskell, Albert L. *Haskell's Historical Guide Book of Somerville, Massachusetts*. Somerville, MA: A.L. Haskell, ca. 1905.

Historic Leave. Somerville Historical Society, 1903–1915.

Hunnewell, James F. *A Century of Town Life: A History of Charlestown, Massachusetts, 1775–1887*. Boston: Little, Brown and Co., 1888.

Karlsen, Carol. *Devil in the Shape of a Woman: Witchcraft in Colonial New England*. New York: Norton, 1987.

Lund, Frederick J. *Brief History of Somerville, 1600–1942*. Somerville, MA: City of Somerville Planning Department, 1996.

Morrison, Ernest P. *Play Ball!: A Memoir of Somerville Baseball*. N.p., 2001.

The Radiator (Somerville High School Yearbook), 1890–1941.

Samuels, Edward A., and Henry H. Kimball. *Somerville, Past and Present: An Illustrated Souvenir*. Boston: Samuels and Kimball, 1897.

Schouler, William. *A History of Massachusetts in the Civil War*. Boston: Dutton, 1868.

Somerville, City of. *Annual Report of Town, Somerville City Directories*, 1842–1930.

The Story of Mary's Little Lamb: as told by Mary and her Neighbors and Friends. Sudbury, MA: Longfellow Wayside Inn, 1928.

Trowbridge, John Townsend. *My Own Story*. Boston: Houghton, Mifflin and Co., 1904.

Zellie, Carole, ed. *Beyond the Neck: The Architecture and Development of Somerville, Massachusetts*. Cambridge, MA: Landscape Research, 1982.

Index

About the Authors

Dee Morris is an independent scholar and educational consultant specializing in nineteenth-century American history and culture. Actively involved in local history projects for over ten years, Dee specializes in lectures and educational programs at Mount Auburn Cemetery in Cambridge, Forest Hills Cemetery in Jamaica Plain and local libraries.

Dora St. Martin is the former head of reference and local history at the Somerville Public Library. For ten years, Dee and Dora have presented walking tours, lectures and exhibits in Somerville and neighboring communities. They have collaborated on *Life in the 90s: The Victorians and Us*, *In Pleasant Company—A Gathering of Choice Spirits: Exploring the Works of John Townsend Trowbridge and Walt Whitman* and "The Art of Prospect Hill, Somerville," an exhibition inviting artists to explore themes in Somerville's past.

Visit us at
www.historypress.net